God's Promises SALO Devotional

DAWN SIMMONS

Weekly Devotional Table of Contents

This Devotional uses 31 of God's Promises from the Bible and is designed as a weekly format with each week having one focus Promise. There is also a prompter question or discussion point to help you get focused on how to apply the Promise to your daily life. The remainder of the week you will be prompted using the SALO (Stop, Ask, Listen, Obey) method with each day focusing one one aspect of SALO. You will also be able to journal your thoughts each day. The SALO method is discussed in depth in my book:

Loving Conversations: How to Pray and Hear God's Voice.

Even if you haven't read the book, this Devotional format is easy to follow and helps you to reflect on Him throughout your week and develop your relationship with Him.

Nothing Can Separate us From God's Love!

Romans 8:35

As you start this week, think about all the times God has shown you His love, even when you felt you didn't deserve it.

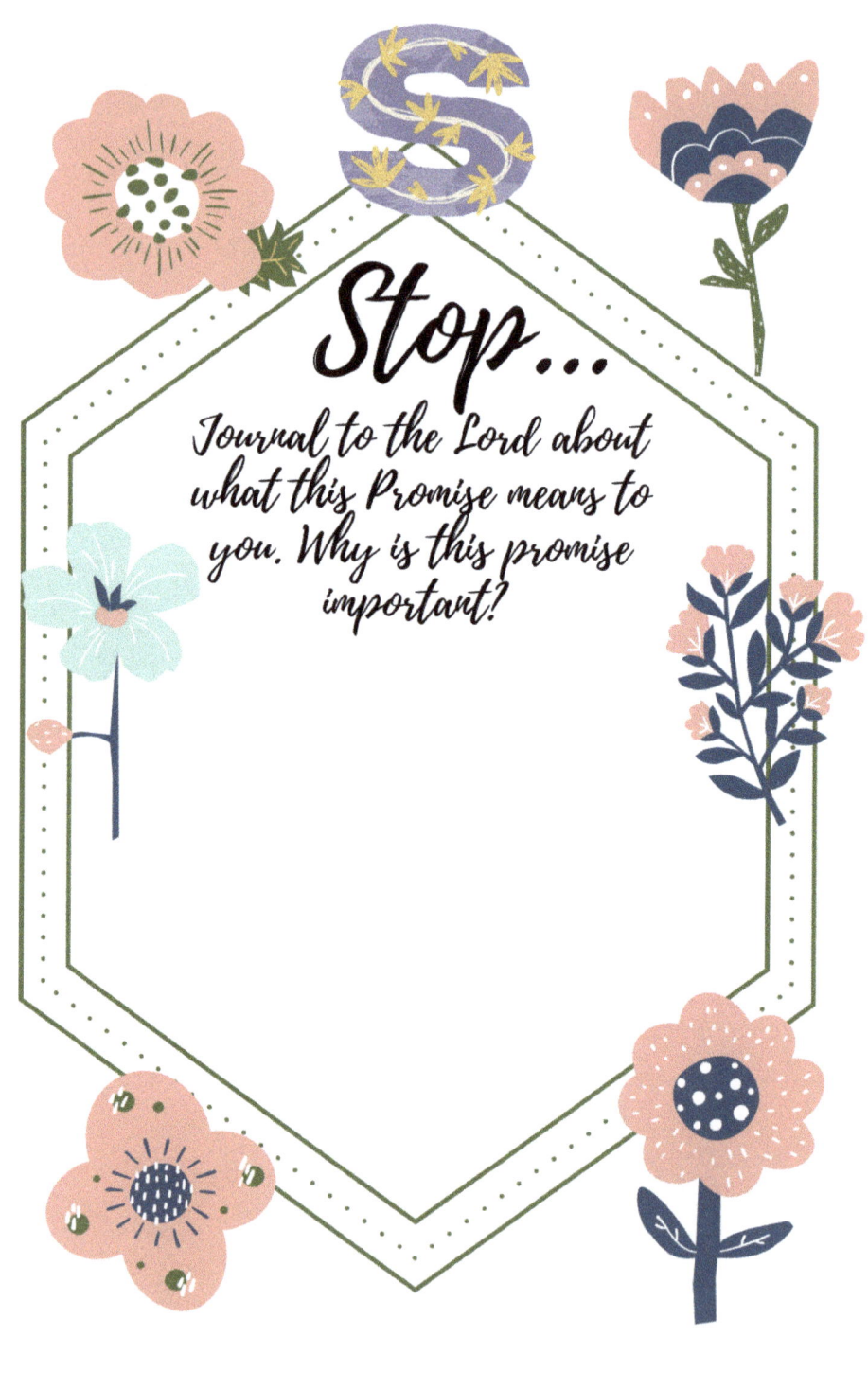

Stop...

Journal to the Lord about what this Promise means to you. Why is this promise important?

A

Ask...

Ask the Lord about how this
Promise applies to your life right
now. Speak from the heart about
why you are asking.

Listen...

Lord, tell me what you have to say about how your Promise applies to me.

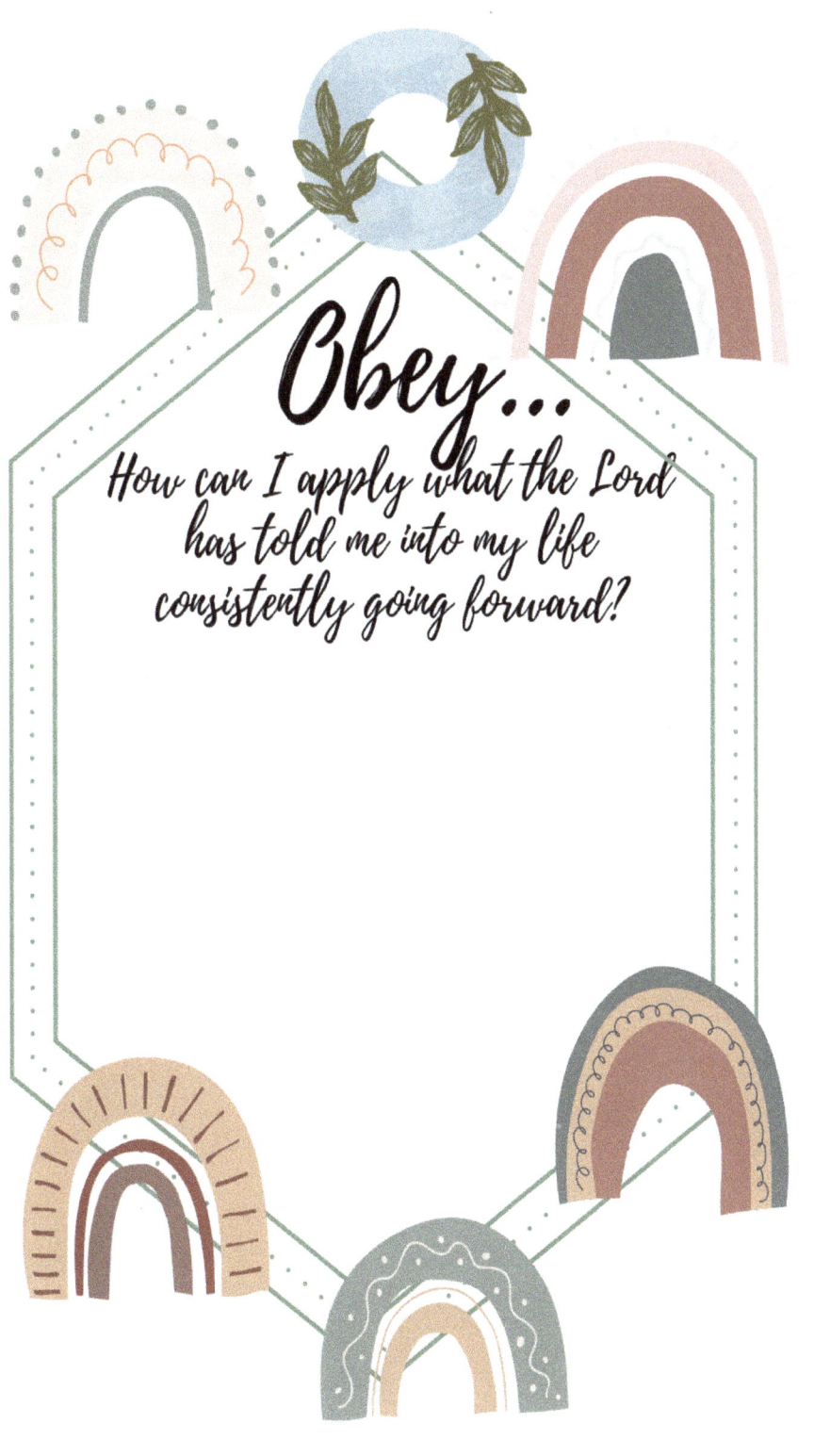

Obey...

How can I apply what the Lord has told me into my life consistently going forward?

If any of you lacks wisdom, you should ask God, who gives generously to all without finding fault, and it will be given to you.

James 1:5

This week really focus on those times you know God gave you guidance and how can you live your life like that everyday with Him.

Stop...

Journal to the Lord about what this Promise means to you. Why is this promise important?

Ask...

Ask the Lord about how this Promise applies to your life right now. Speak from the heart about why you are asking.

L

Listen...

Lord, tell me what you have to say about how your Promise applies to me.

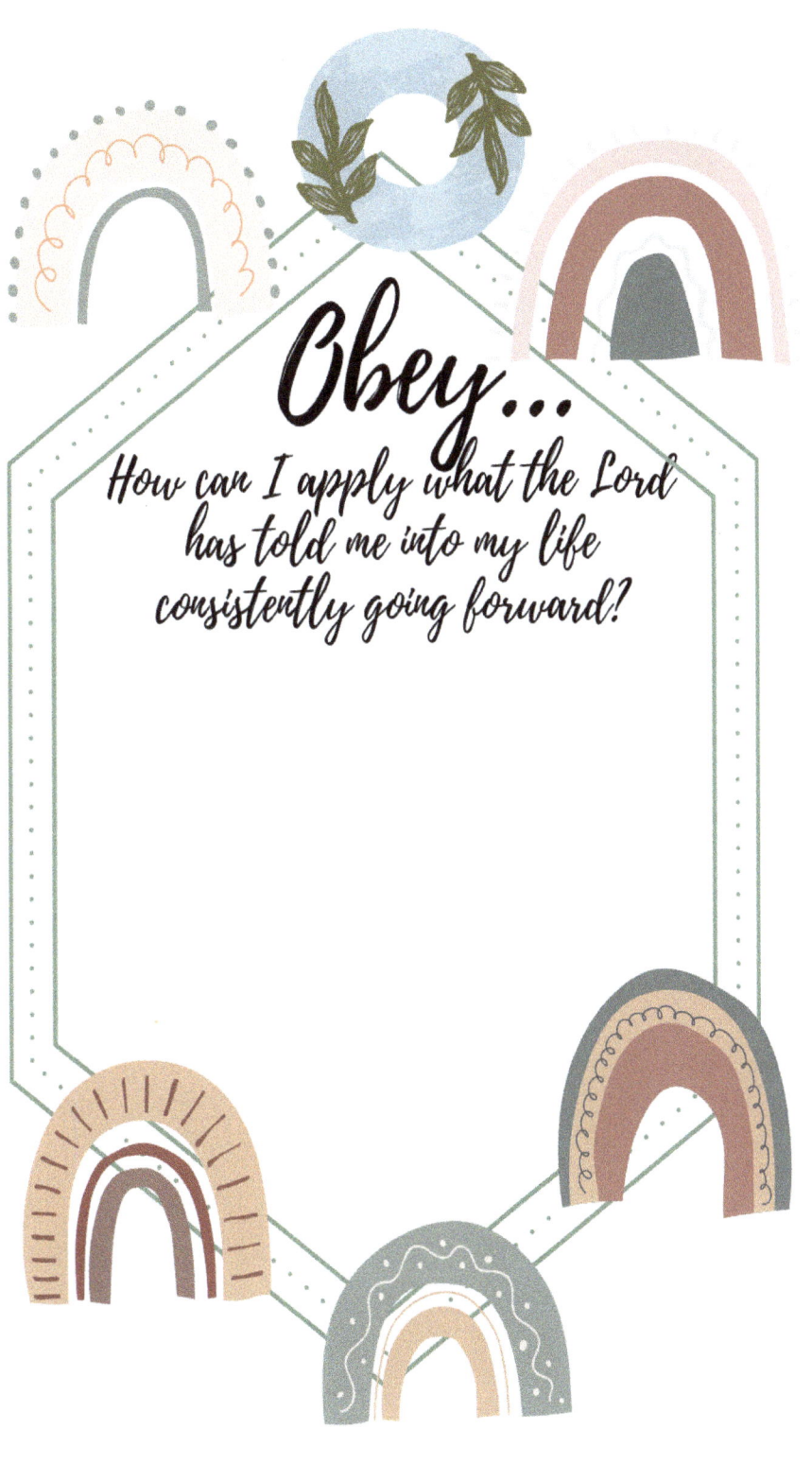

Obey...

How can I apply what the Lord has told me into my life consistently going forward?

Then you will call on me and come and pray to me, and I will listen to you.

Jeremiah 29:12

When you are in need, do you call on the Lord first? How can you develop your heart to make Him your first response in times of need?

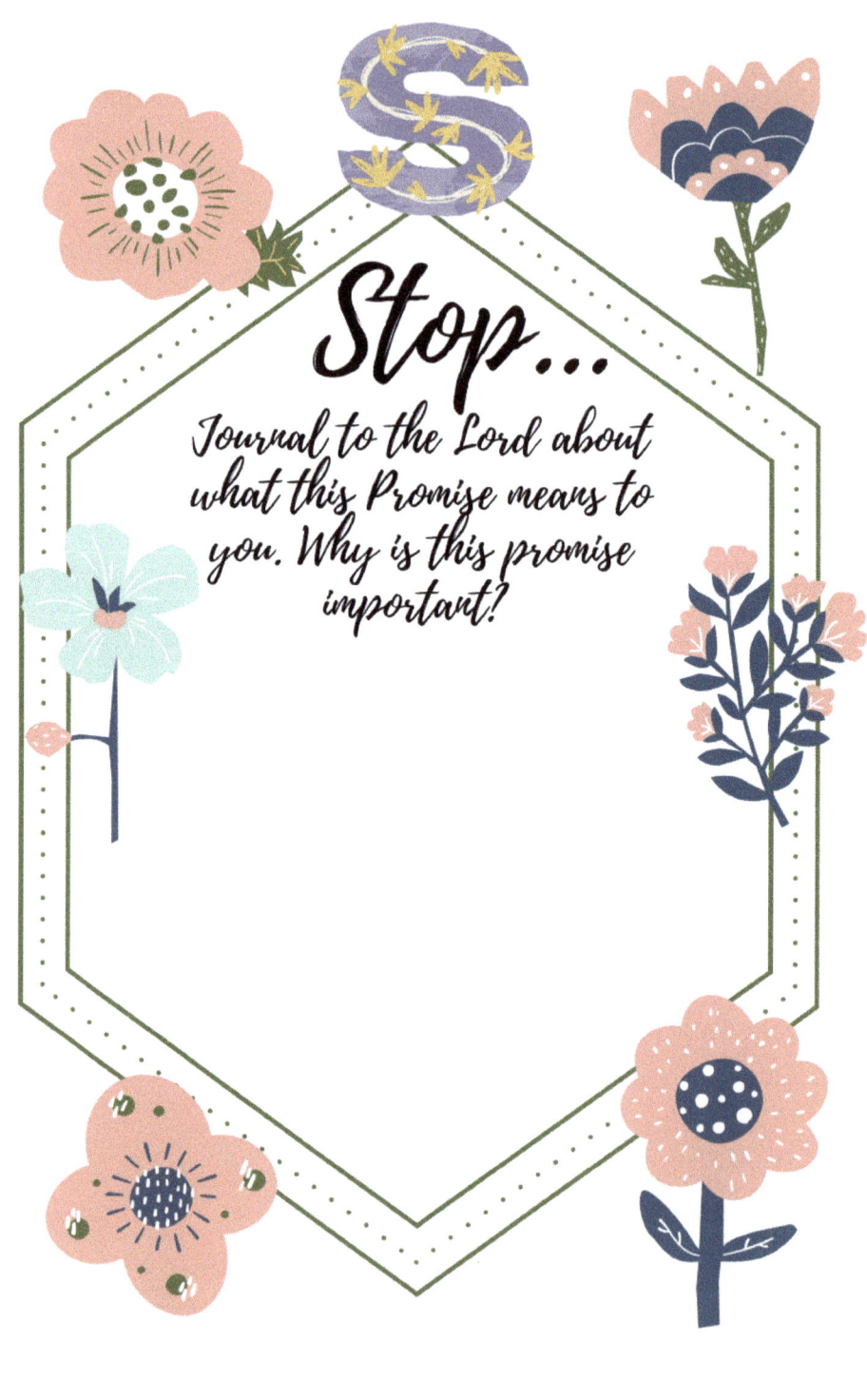

Stop...

Journal to the Lord about what this Promise means to you. Why is this promise important?

Ask...

Ask the Lord about how this Promise applies to your life right now. Speak from the heart about why you are asking.

Listen...

Lord, tell me what you have
to say about how your
Promise applies to me.

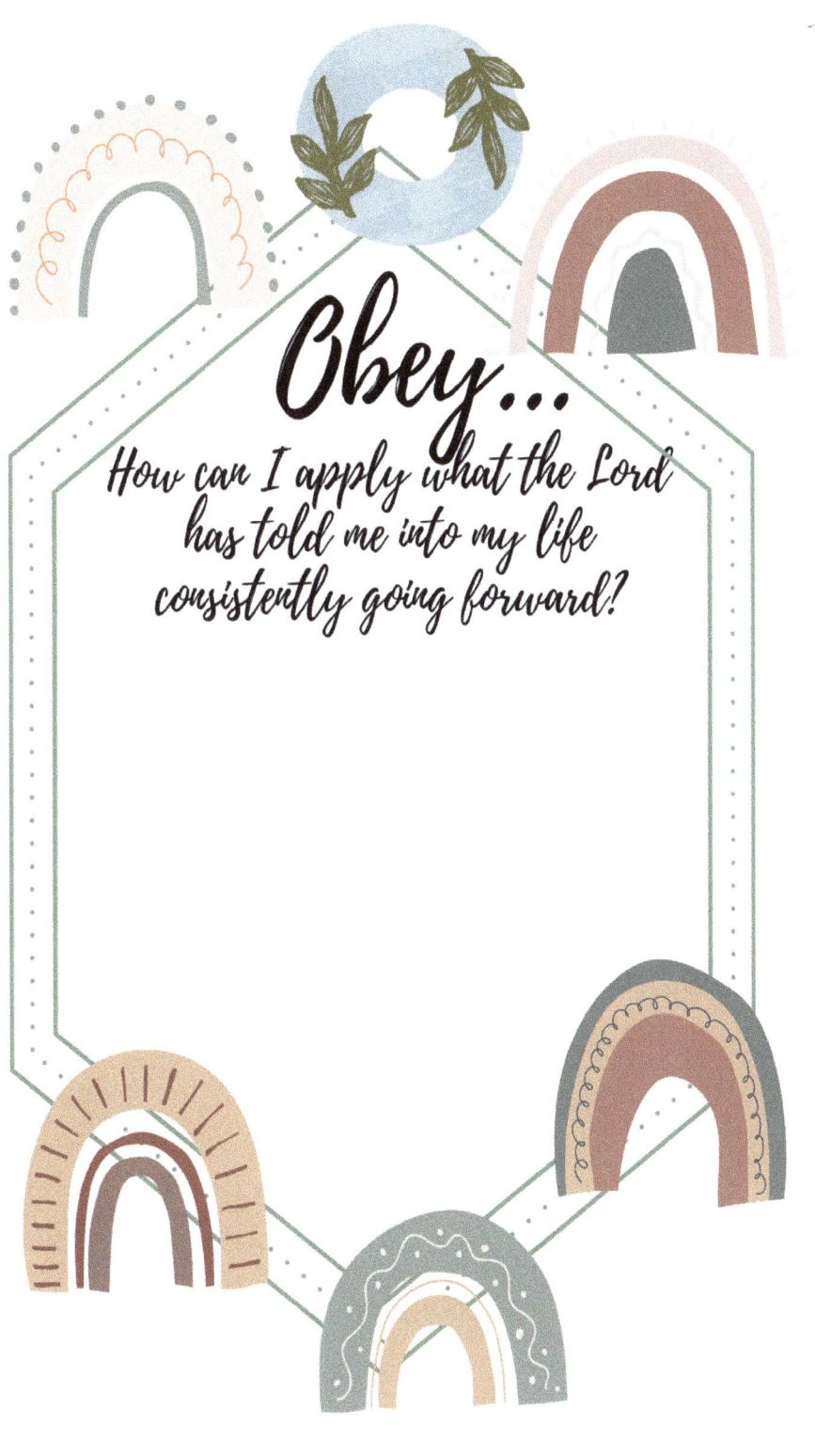

Obey...

How can I apply what the Lord has told me into my life consistently going forward?

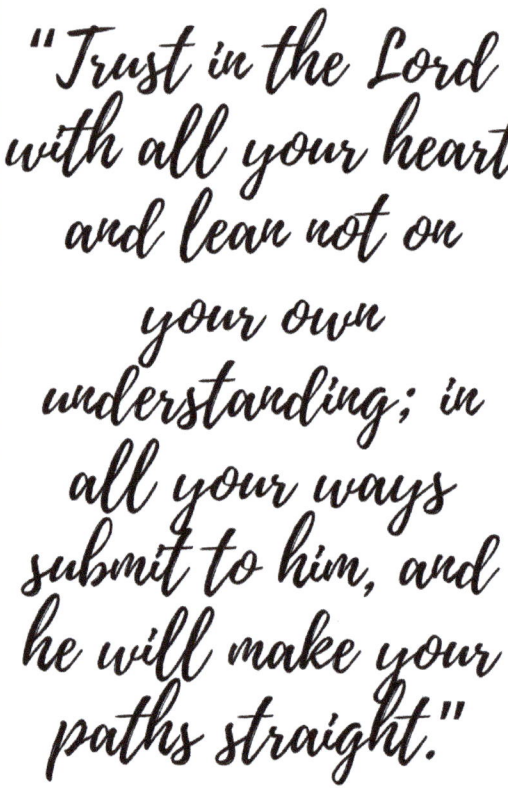

"Trust in the Lord with all your heart and lean not on your own understanding; in all your ways submit to him, and he will make your paths straight."

Prov 3:5-6

What has held you back from fully trusting in God? Do you trust only what you can see? Are you willing to submit fully to Him?

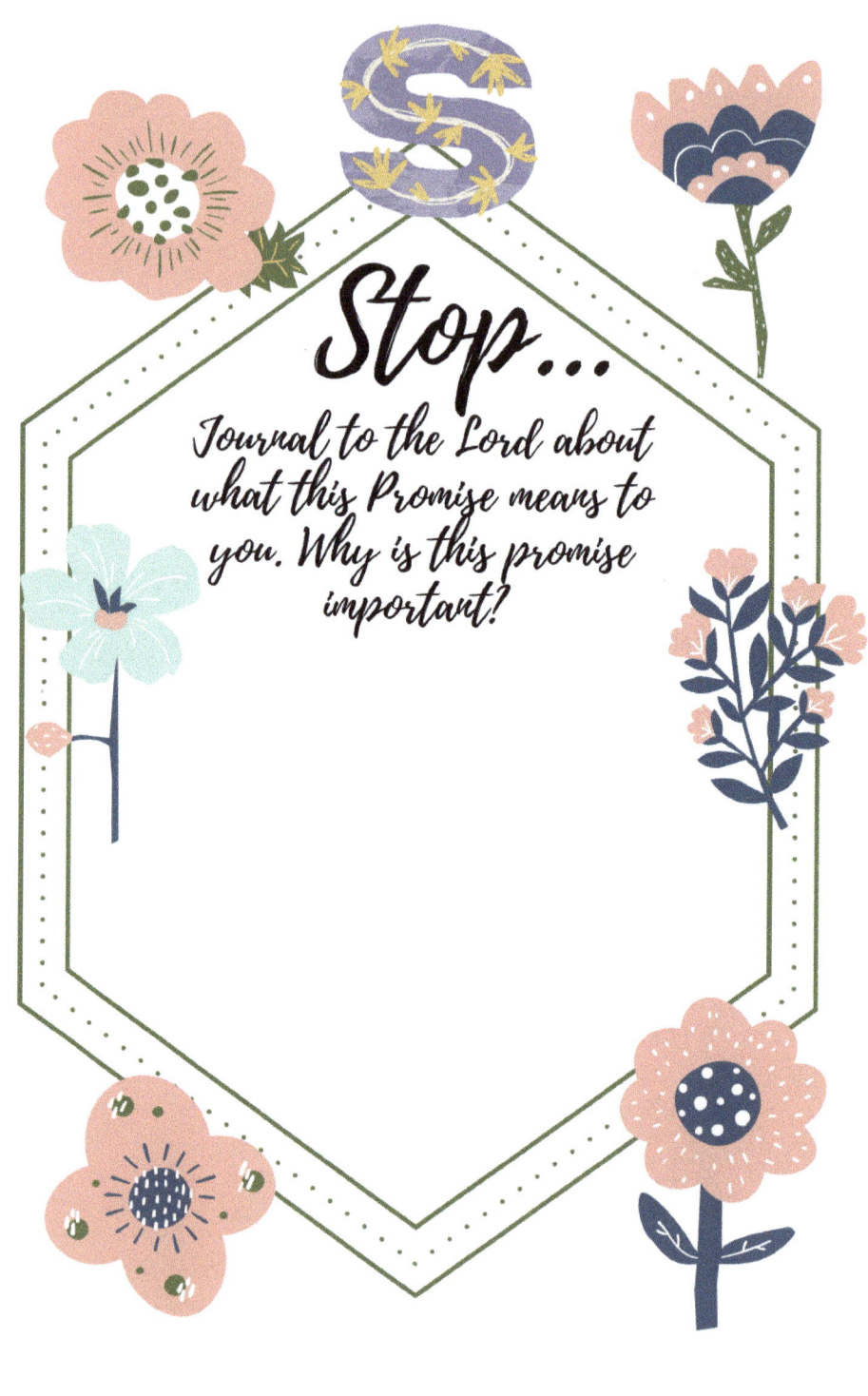

Stop...

Journal to the Lord about what this Promise means to you. Why is this promise important?

Ask...

Ask the Lord about how this Promise applies to your life right now. Speak from the heart about why you are asking.

Listen...

Lord, tell me what you have
to say about how your
Promise applies to me.

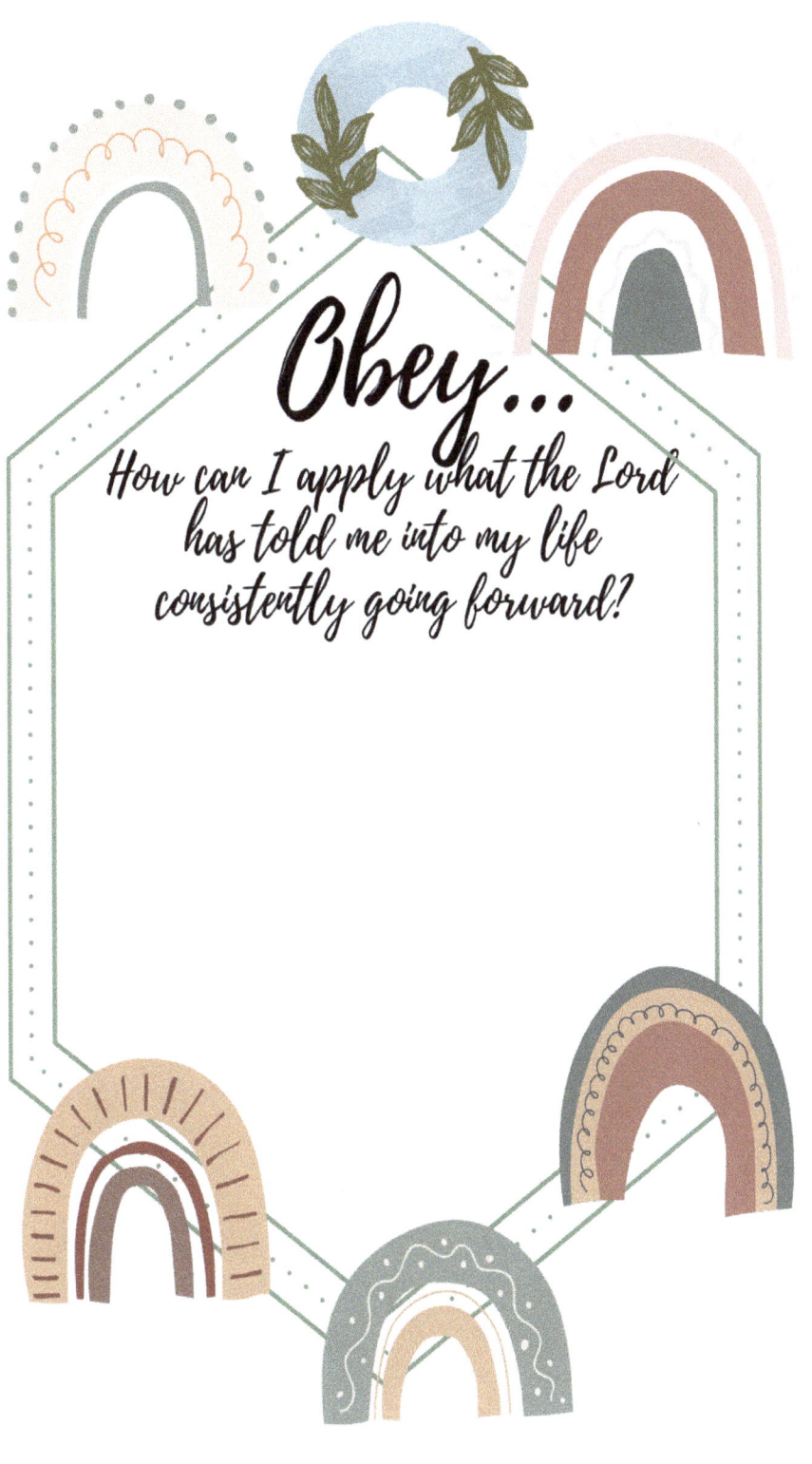

Obey...

How can I apply what the Lord has told me into my life consistently going forward?

Take delight in the Lord, and he will give you the desires of your heart.

Ps 37:4

Do you truly believe God is willing to give you the desires of your heart? When was the last time you took delight in the Lord?

Stop...

Journal to the Lord about what this Promise means to you. Why is this promise important?

Ask...

Ask the Lord about how this Promise applies to your life right now. Speak from the heart about why you are asking.

L

Listen...

Lord, tell me what you have
to say about how your
Promise applies to me.

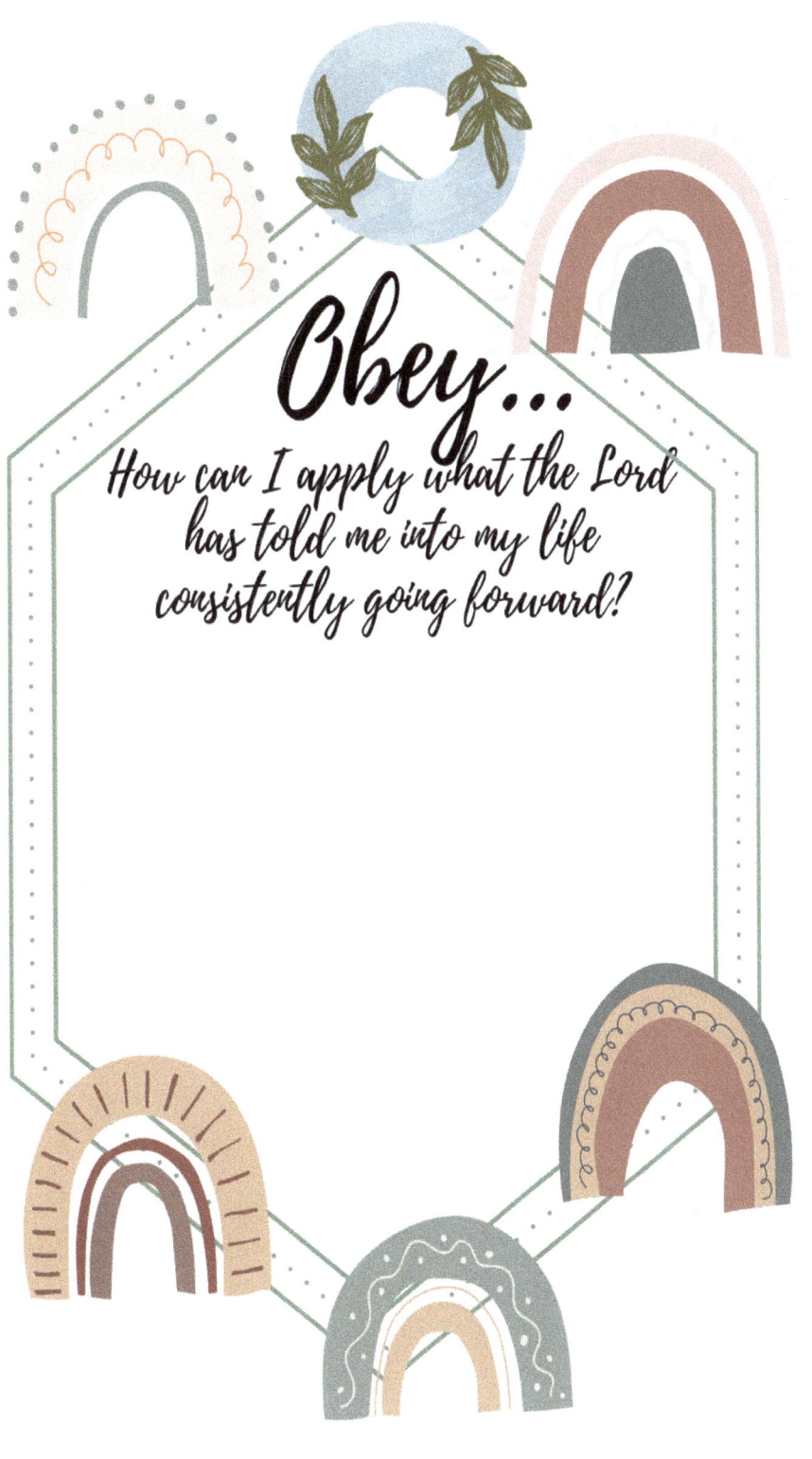

Obey...

How can I apply what the Lord has told me into my life consistently going forward?

And God is able
to bless you
abundantly, so
that in all
things at all
times, having all
that you need,
you will abound
in every good
work.

2 Cor 9:8

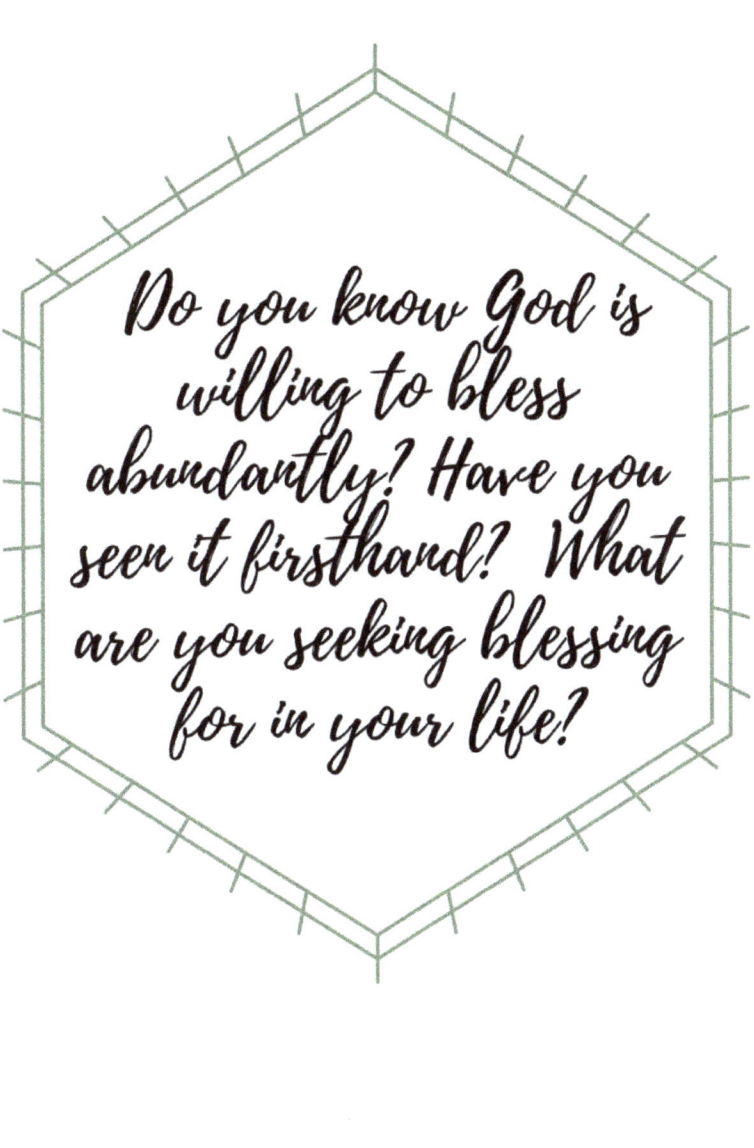

Do you know God is willing to bless abundantly? Have you seen it firsthand? What are you seeking blessing for in your life?

Stop...

Journal to the Lord about what this Promise means to you. Why is this promise important?

Ask...

Ask the Lord about how this Promise applies to your life right now. Speak from the heart about why you are asking.

L

Listen...

Lord, tell me what you have to say about how your Promise applies to me.

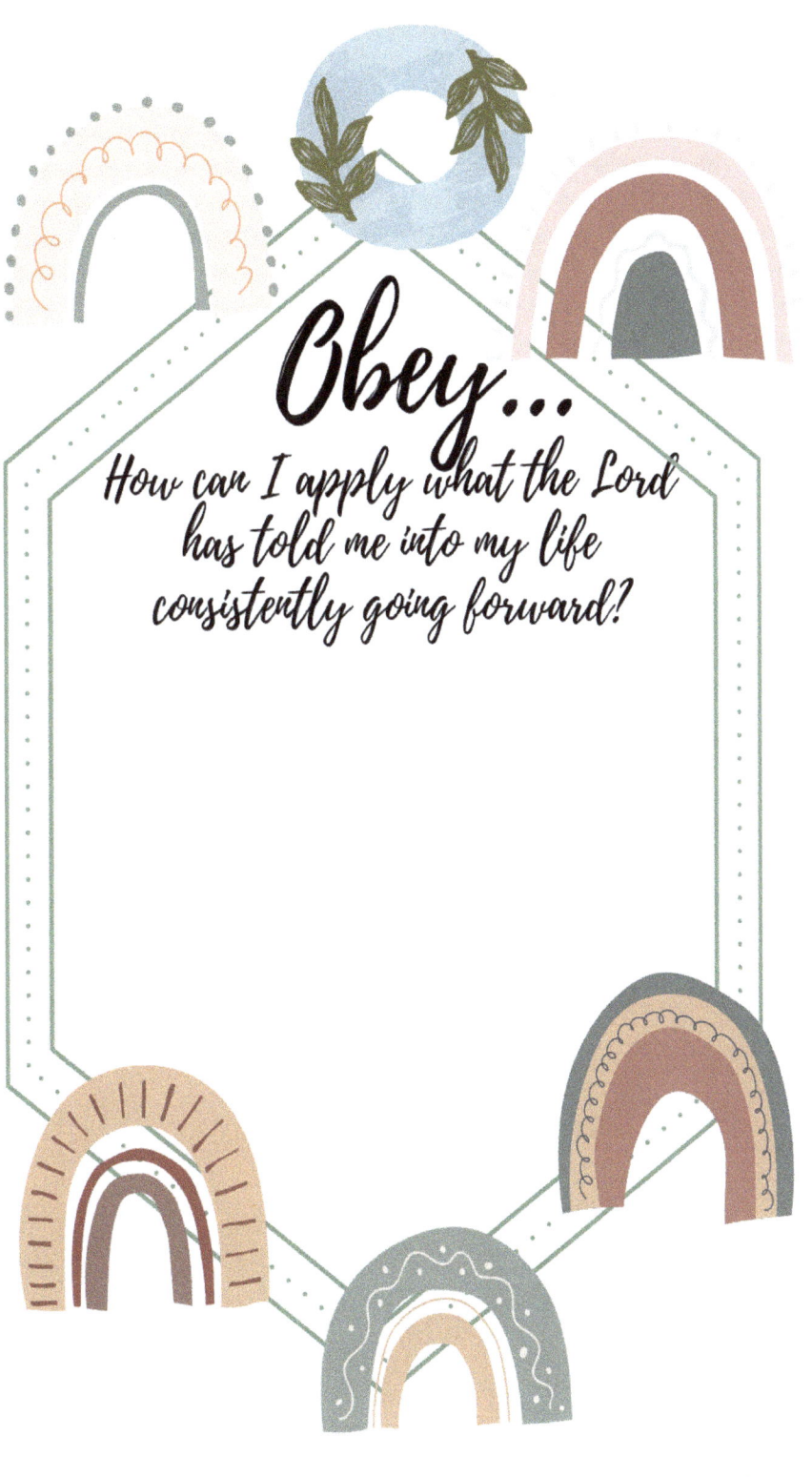

Obey...

How can I apply what the Lord has told me into my life consistently going forward?

Which of you, if your son asks for bread, will give him a stone? Or if he asks for a fish, will give him a snake? If you, then, though you are evil, know how to give good gifts to your children, how much more will your Father in heaven give good gifts to those who ask him!

Mt 7:9-11

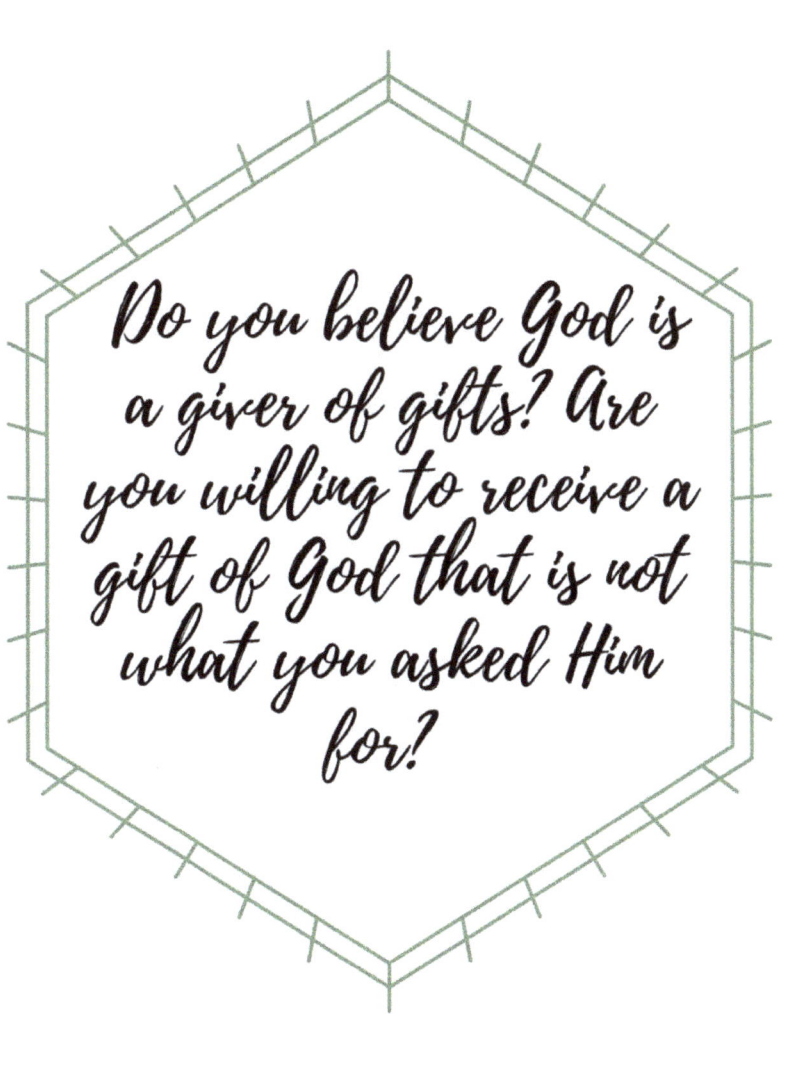

Do you believe God is a giver of gifts? Are you willing to receive a gift of God that is not what you asked Him for?

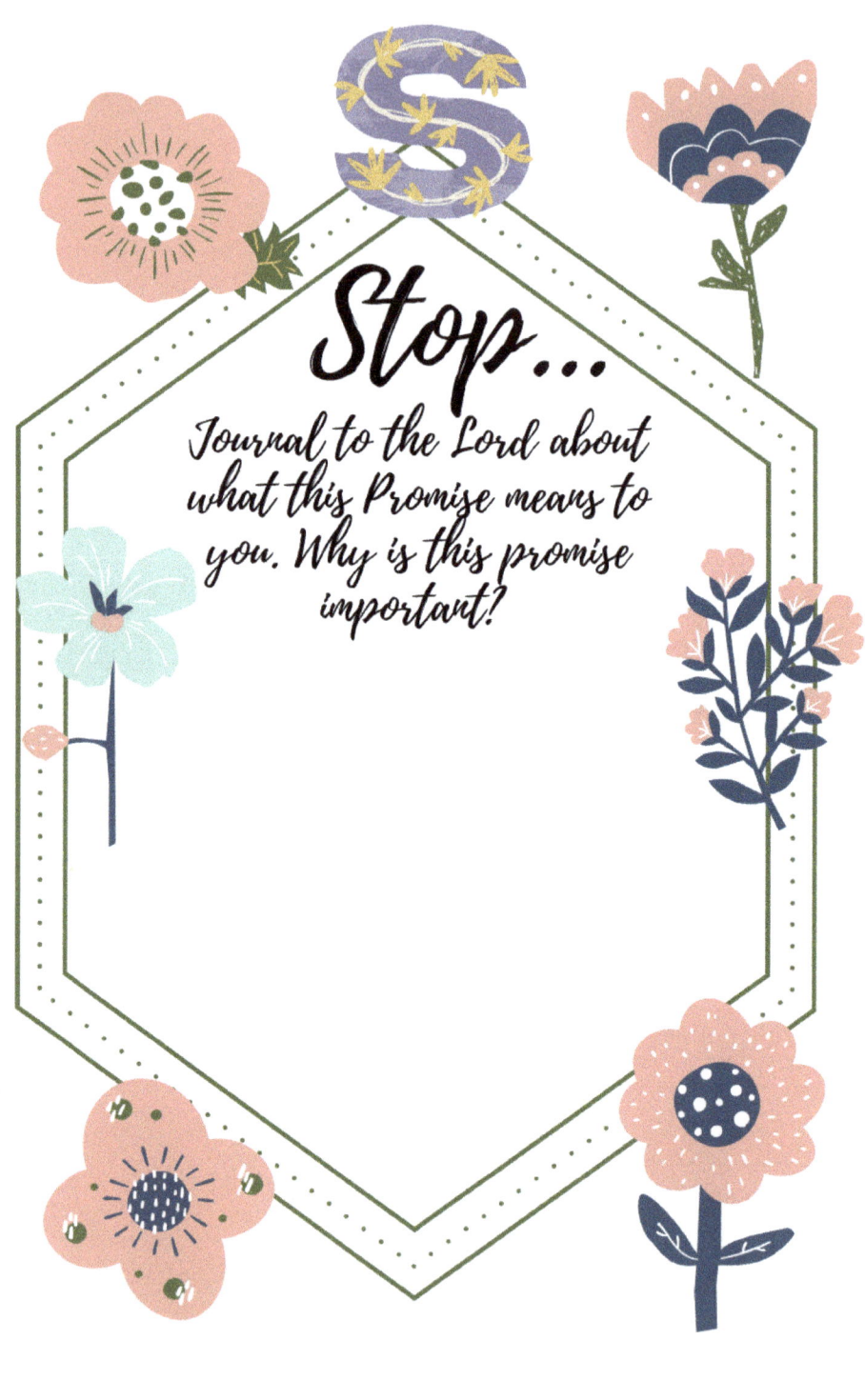

Stop...

Journal to the Lord about what this Promise means to you. Why is this promise important?

A

Ask...

Ask the Lord about how this Promise applies to your life right now. Speak from the heart about why you are asking.

Listen...

Lord, tell me what you have to say about how your Promise applies to me.

Obey...

How can I apply what the Lord has told me into my life consistently going forward?

When you pass through the waters, I will be with you; and when you pass through the rivers, they will not sweep over you. When you walk through the fire, you will not be burned; the flames will not set you ablaze.

Is 43:2

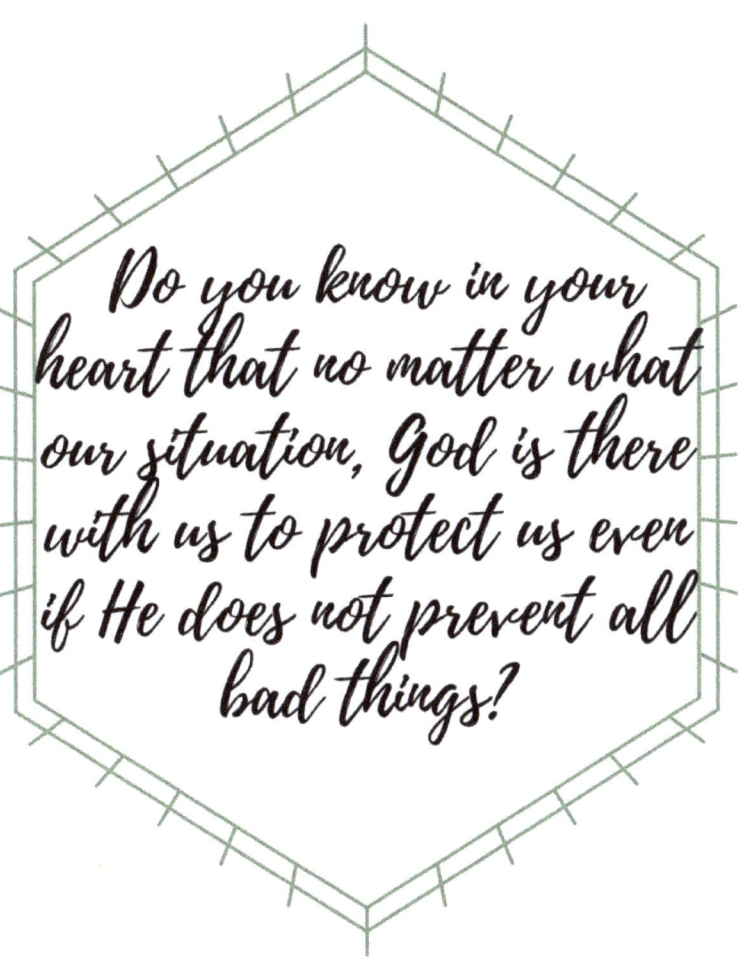

Do you know in your heart that no matter what our situation, God is there with us to protect us even if He does not prevent all bad things?

Stop...

Journal to the Lord about what this Promise means to you. Why is this promise important?

A

Ask...

Ask the Lord about how this Promise applies to your life right now. Speak from the heart about why you are asking.

Listen...

Lord, tell me what you have to say about how your Promise applies to me.

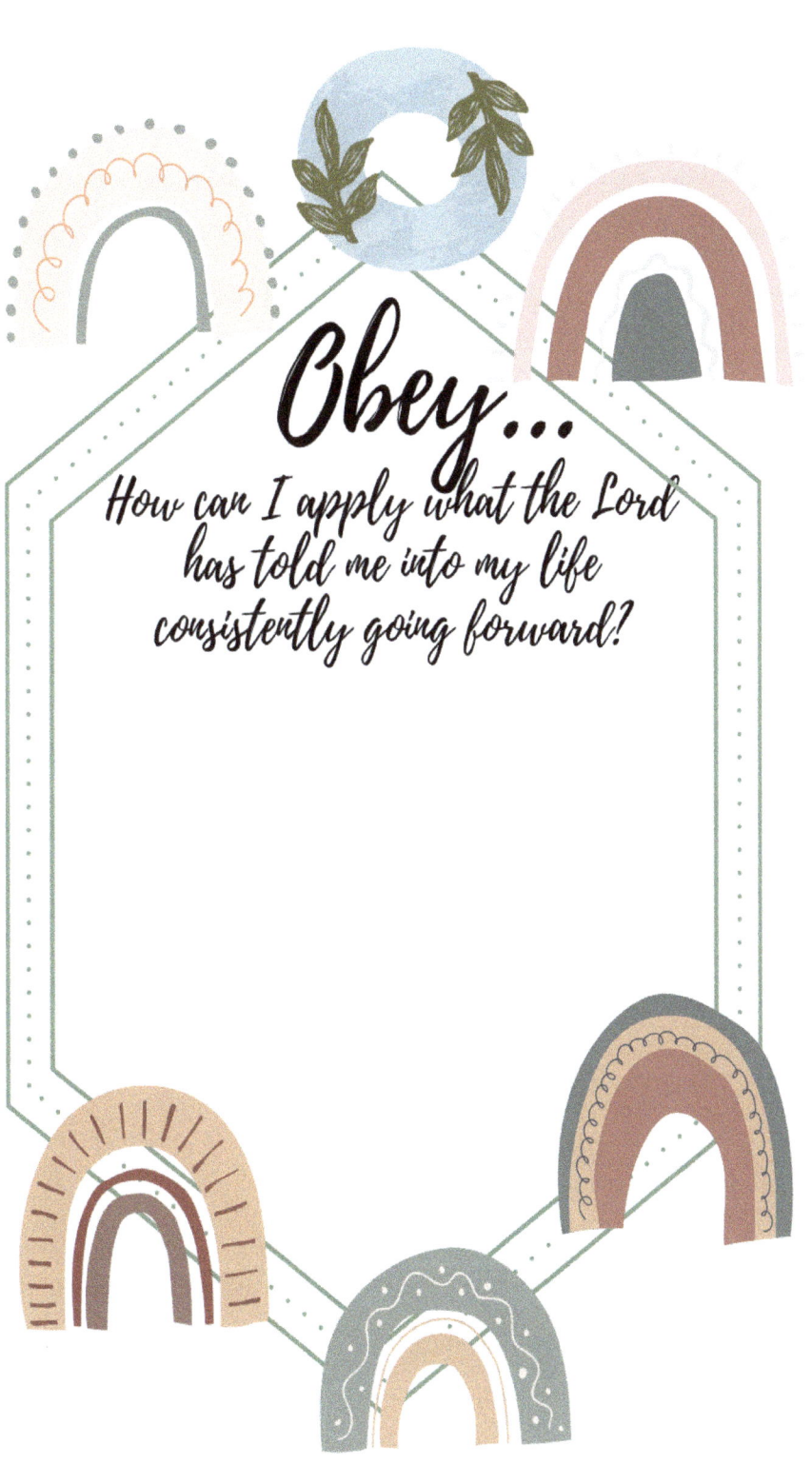

Obey...

How can I apply what the Lord has told me into my life consistently going forward?

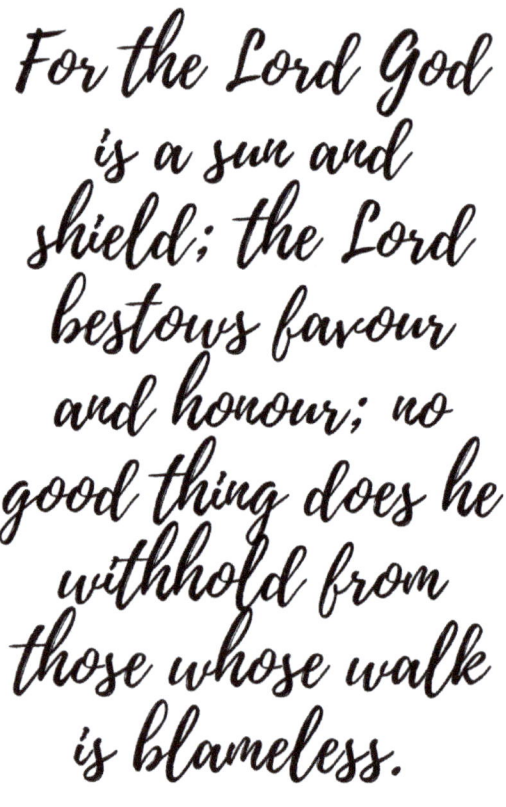

For the Lord God is a sun and shield; the Lord bestows favour and honour; no good thing does he withhold from those whose walk is blameless.

Ps 84:11

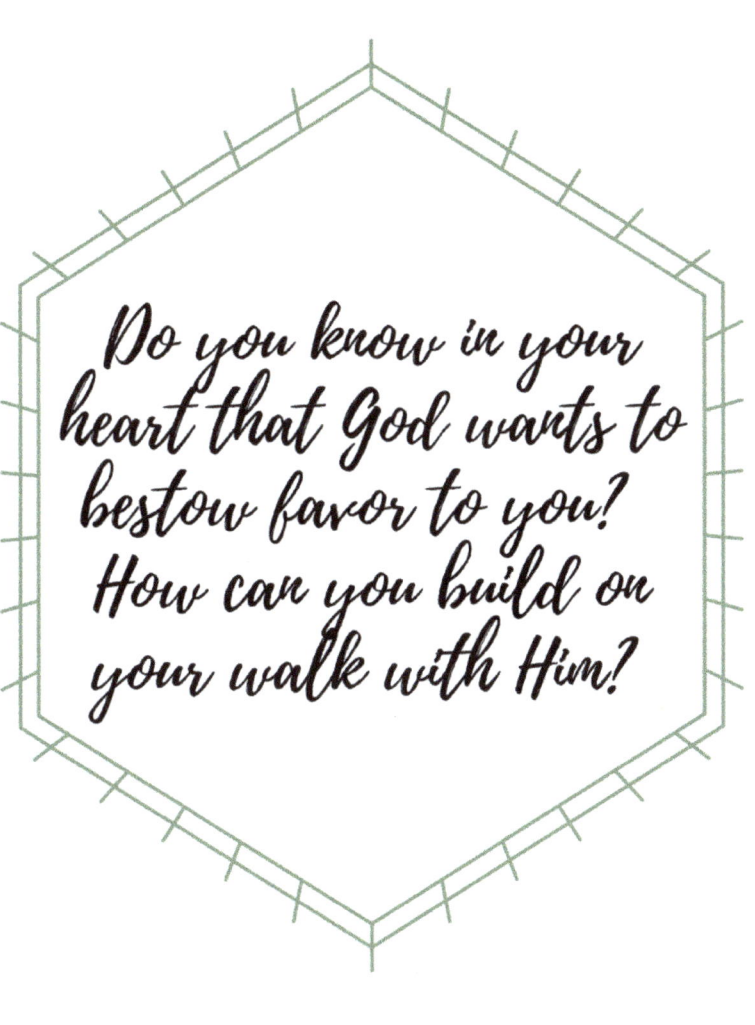

Do you know in your heart that God wants to bestow favor to you? How can you build on your walk with Him?

Stop...

Journal to the Lord about what this Promise means to you. Why is this promise important?

Ask...

Ask the Lord about how this Promise applies to your life right now. Speak from the heart about why you are asking.

L

Listen...

Lord, tell me what you have
to say about how your
Promise applies to me.

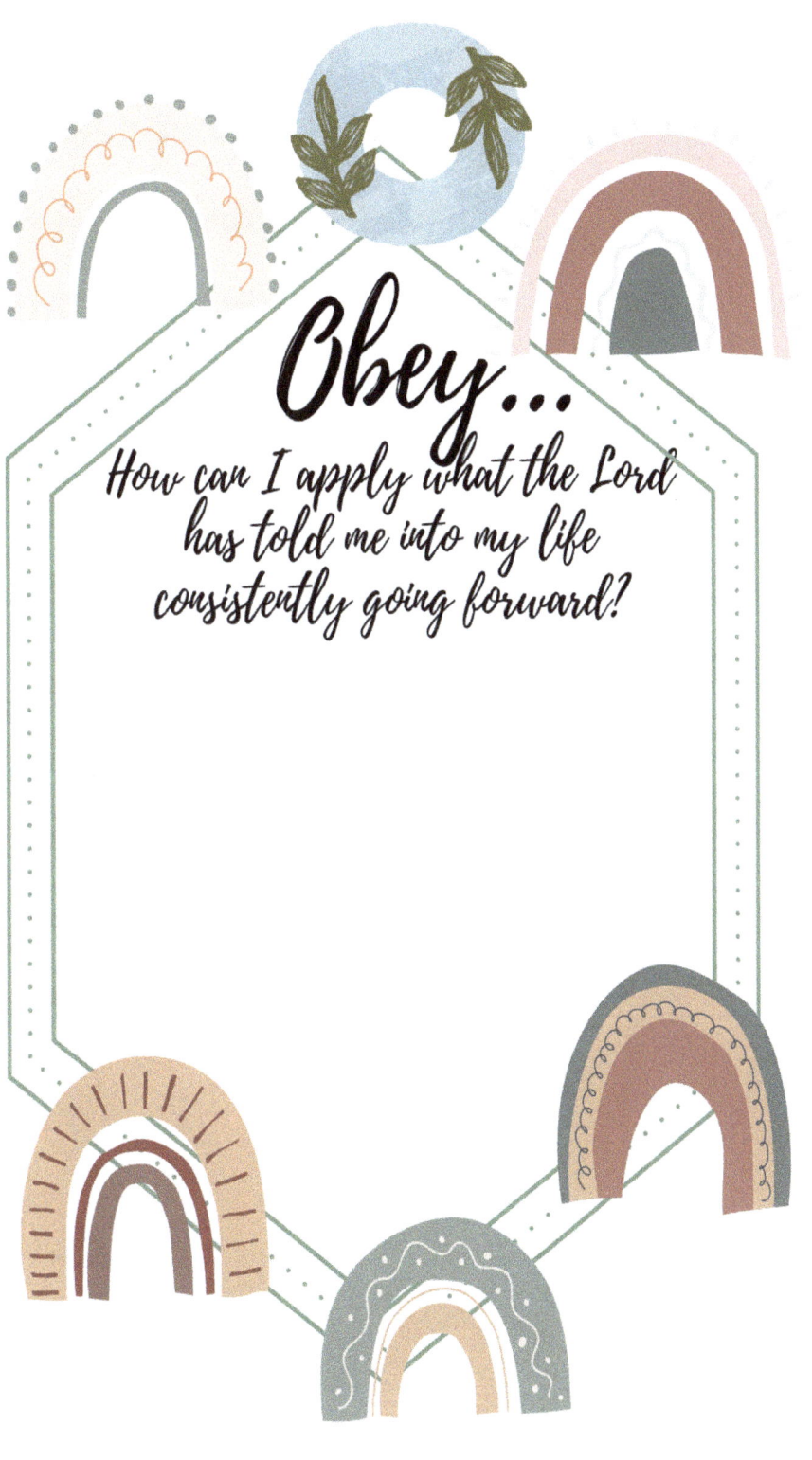

Obey...

How can I apply what the Lord has told me into my life consistently going forward?

The lions may grow weak and hungry, but those who seek the Lord lack no good thing.

Ps 34:10

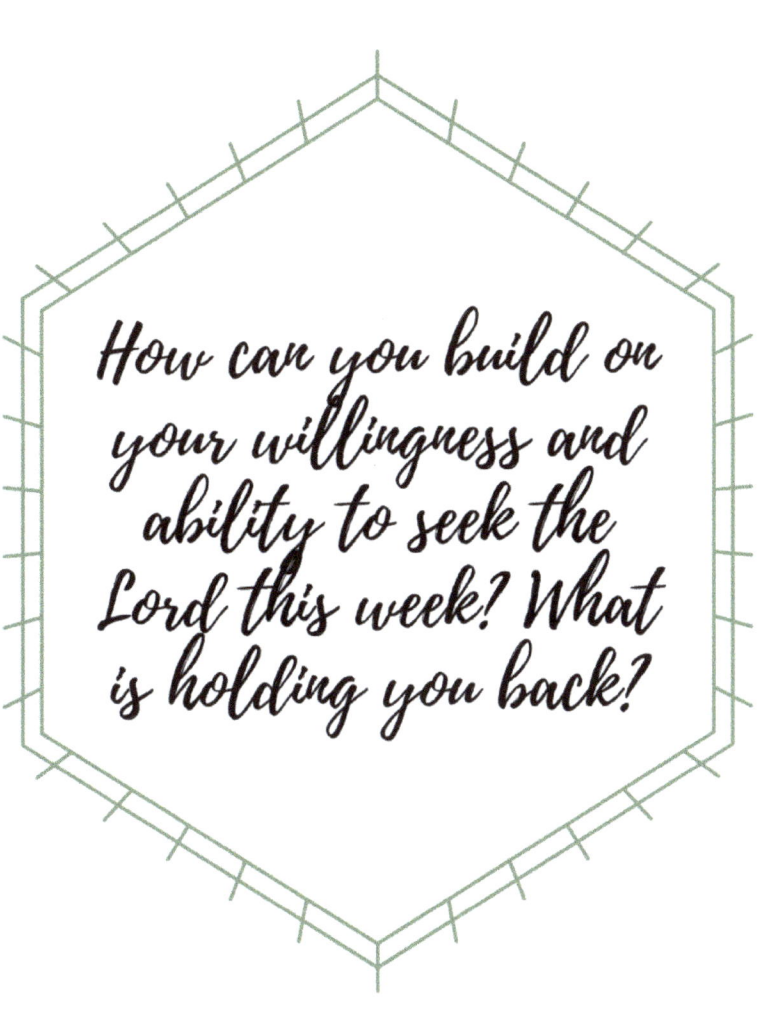

How can you build on your willingness and ability to seek the Lord this week? What is holding you back?

S

Stop...

Journal to the Lord about what this Promise means to you. Why is this promise important?

Ask...

Ask the Lord about how this Promise applies to your life right now. Speak from the heart about why you are asking.

L

Listen...

Lord, tell me what you have to say about how your Promise applies to me.

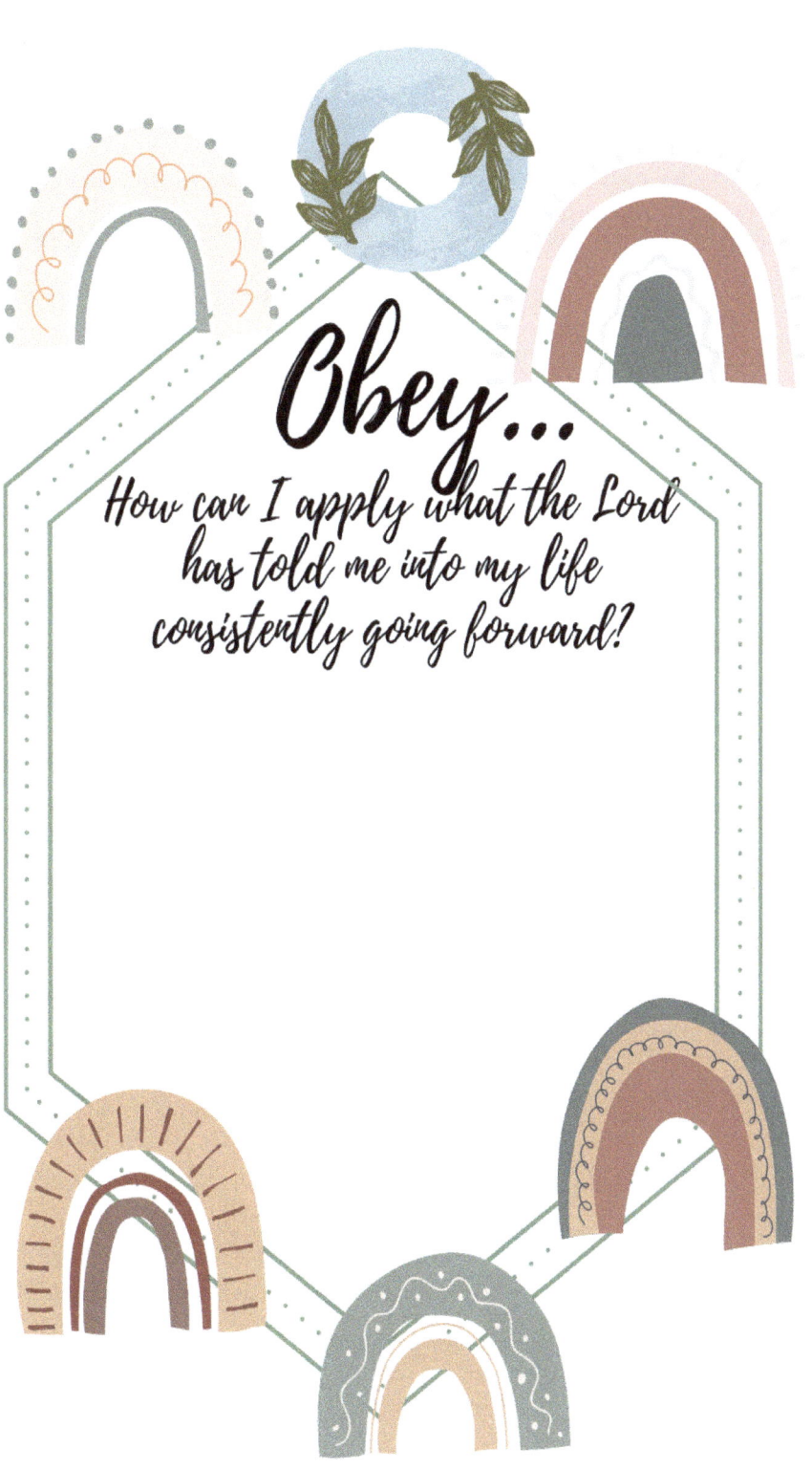

Obey...

How can I apply what the Lord has told me into my life consistently going forward?

The LORD himself goes before you and will be with you; he will never leave you nor forsake you. Do not be afraid; do not be discouraged.

Deut 31:8

This week focus on the times in your life when the Lord went before you. How did he show you His presence so you were not afraid or discouraged?

Stop...

Journal to the Lord about what this Promise means to you. Why is this promise important?

A

Ask...

Ask the Lord about how this Promise applies to your life right now. Speak from the heart about why you are asking.

Listen...

Lord, tell me what you have
to say about how your
Promise applies to me.

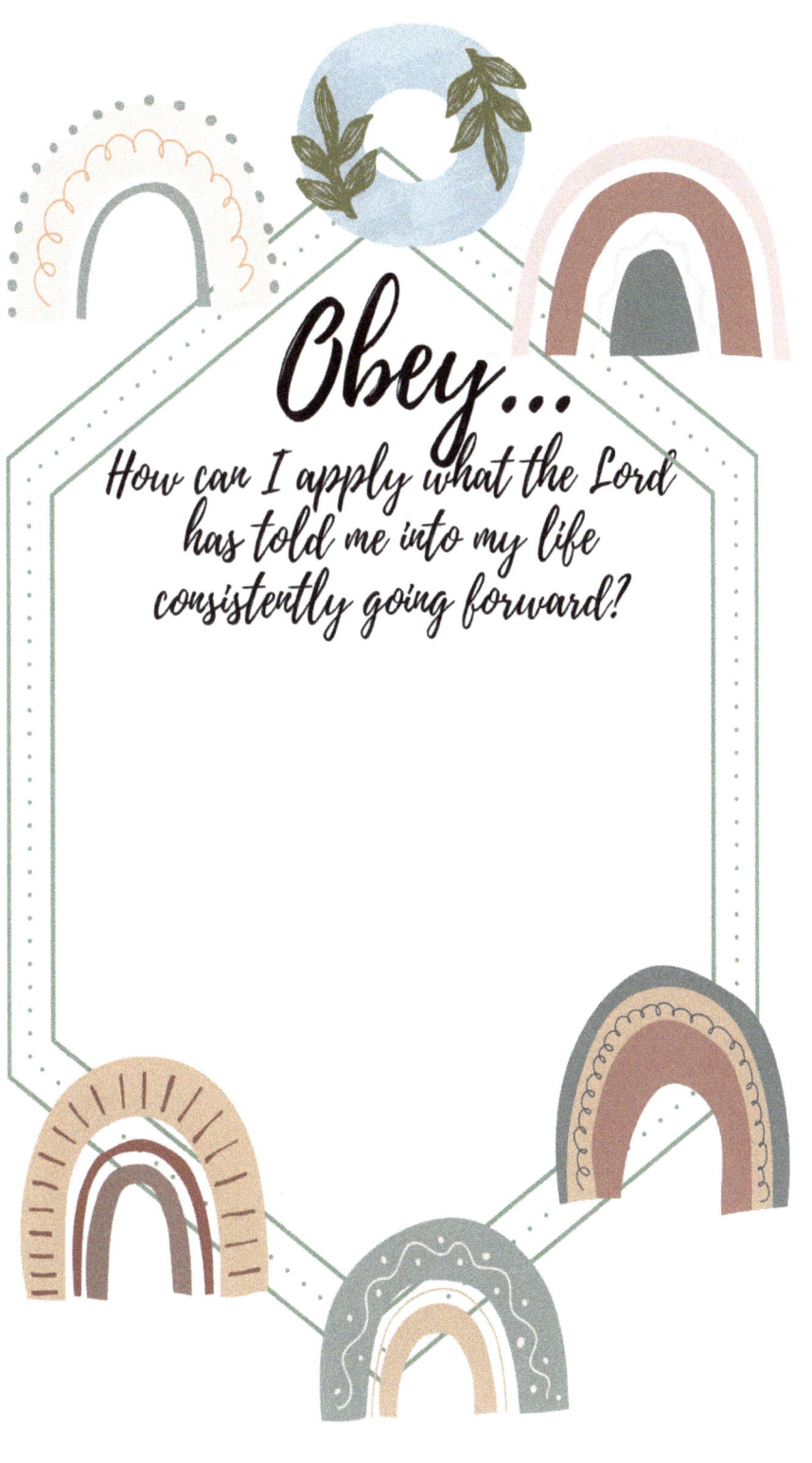

Obey...

How can I apply what the Lord has told me into my life consistently going forward?

Come to me, all you who are weary and burdened, and I will give you rest. Take my yoke upon you and learn from me, for I am gentle and humble in heart, and you will find rest for your souls. For my yoke is easy and my burden is light.

Matthew 11:28-39

Are you willing to seek the Lord when you need rest? Will you let Him bear the burden or do you want to hold onto it and control it?

Stop...

Journal to the Lord about what this Promise means to you. Why is this promise important?

A

Ask...

Ask the Lord about how this Promise applies to your life right now. Speak from the heart about why you are asking.

Listen...

Lord, tell me what you have to say about how your Promise applies to me.

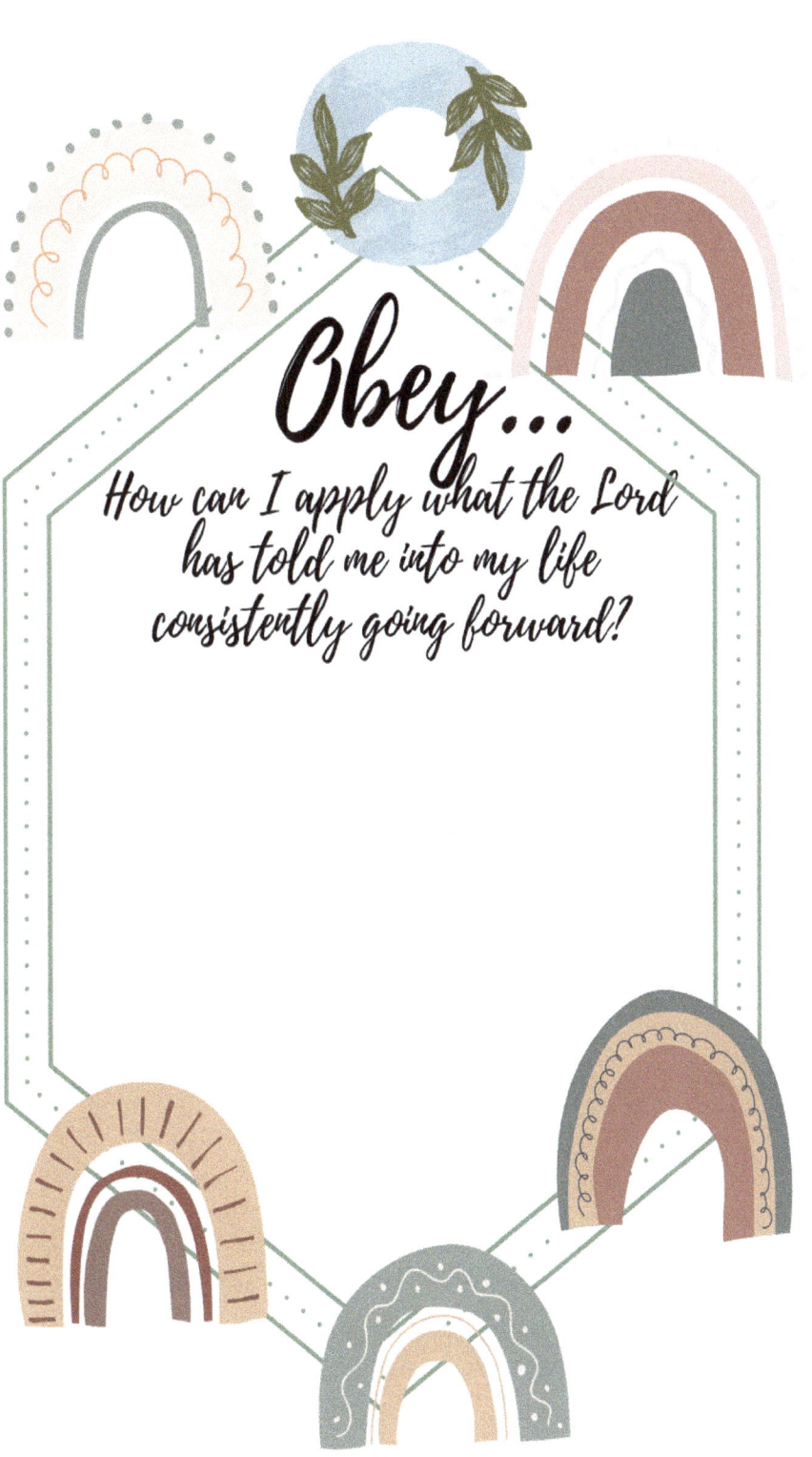

Obey...

How can I apply what the Lord has told me into my life consistently going forward?

So I say to you: Ask and it will be given to you; seek and you will find; knock and the door will be opened to you. For everyone who asks receives; the one who seeks finds; and to the one who knocks, the door will be opened. Which of you fathers, if your son asks for a fish, will give him a snake instead? Or if he asks for an egg, will give him a scorpion? If you then, though you are evil, know how to give good gifts to your children, how much more will your Father in heaven give the Holy Spirit to those who ask him!

Luke 11:9-13

Ask, Seek, Knock requires perseverance. Are you willing to pursue God with perseverance? Has He answered you and you didn't recognize it?

Stop...

Journal to the Lord about what this Promise means to you. Why is this promise important?

A

Ask...

Ask the Lord about how this Promise applies to your life right now. Speak from the heart about why you are asking.

L

Listen...

Lord, tell me what you have
to say about how your
Promise applies to me.

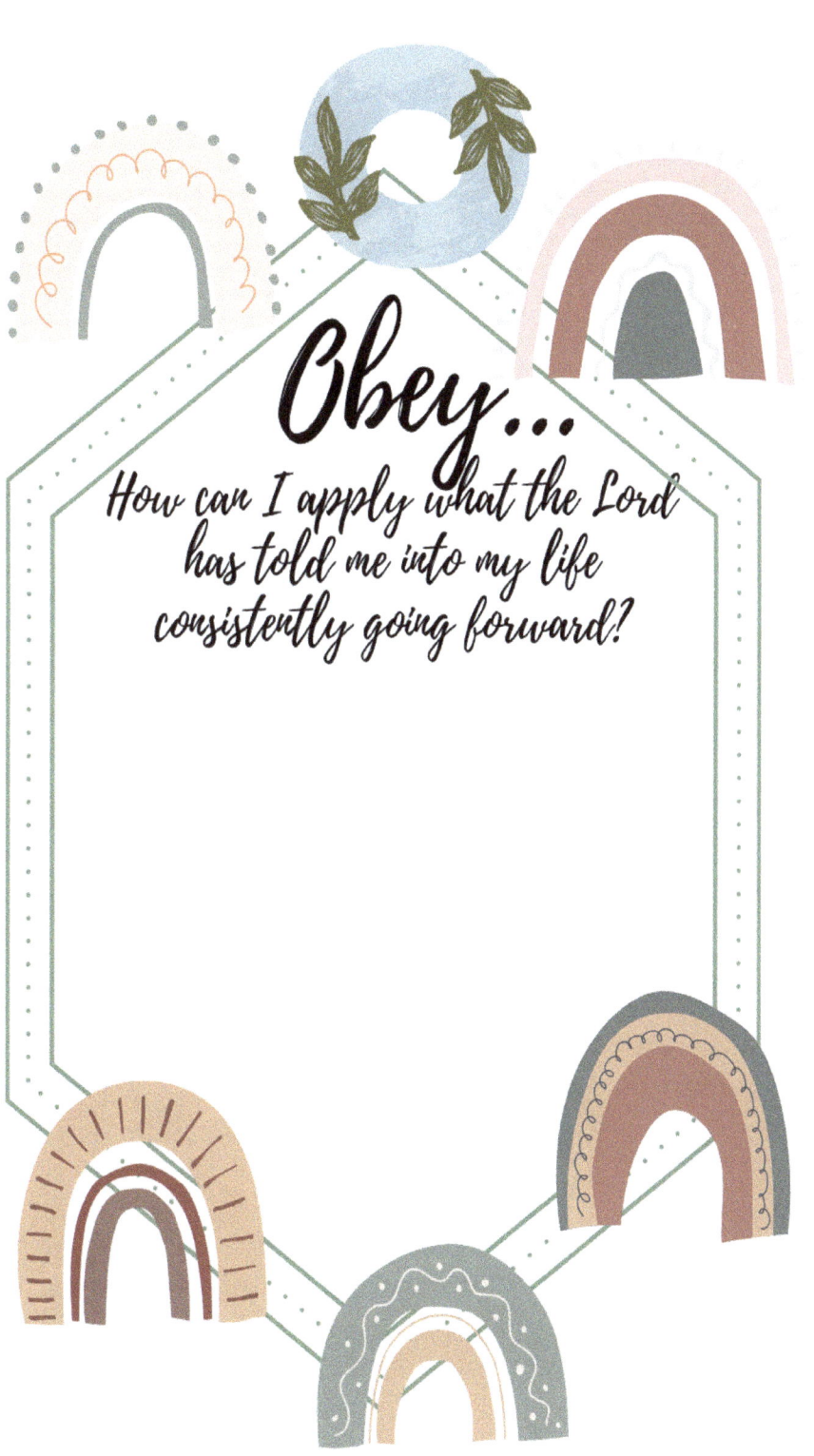

Obey...

How can I apply what the Lord has told me into my life consistently going forward?

Do not let your hearts be troubled. You believe in God; believe also in me. My Father's house has many rooms; if that were not so, would I have told you that I am going there to prepare a place for you? 3 And if I go and prepare a place for you, I will come back and take you to be with me that you also may be where I am.

John 14:1-3

How does it feel knowing there is a place for you in heaven with the Lord? What comes to mind when you think of Him coming back and taking you with Him?

Stop...

Journal to the Lord about what this Promise means to you. Why is this promise important?

Ask...

Ask the Lord about how this Promise applies to your life right now. Speak from the heart about why you are asking.

Listen...

Lord, tell me what you have
to say about how your
Promise applies to me.

Obey...

How can I apply what the Lord has told me into my life consistently going forward?

Peace I leave with you; my peace I give you. I do not give to you as the world gives. Do not let your hearts be troubled and do not be afraid.

John 14:27

How often do you feel God's peace? How can you find develop yourself to be with Him more at peace with His will in your life?

Stop...

Journal to the Lord about what this Promise means to you. Why is this promise important?

A

Ask...

Ask the Lord about how this Promise applies to your life right now. Speak from the heart about why you are asking.

L

Listen...

Lord, tell me what you have to say about how your Promise applies to me.

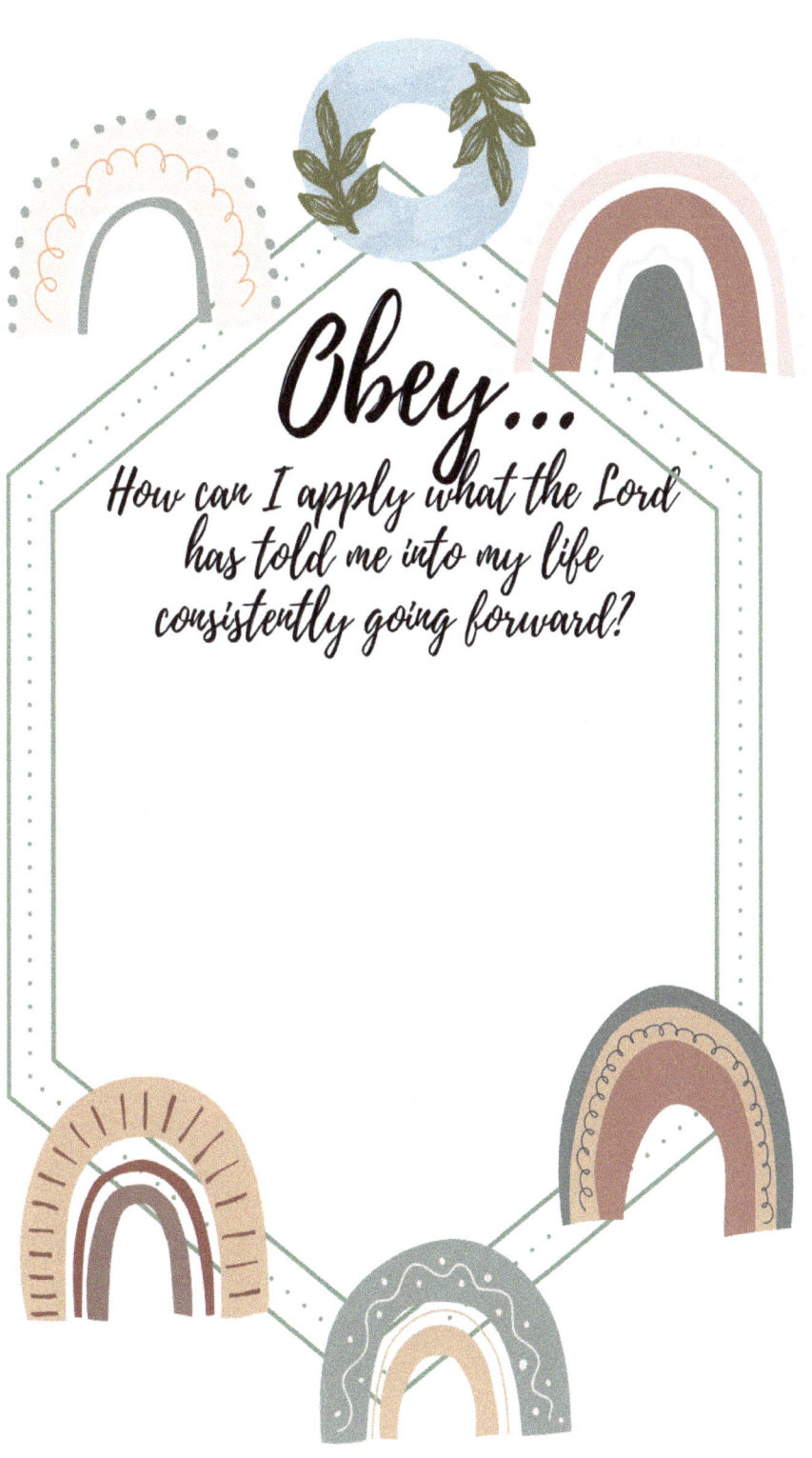

Obey...

How can I apply what the Lord has told me into my life consistently going forward?

I am the light of the world. Whoever follows me will never walk in darkness, but will have the light of life.

John 8:12

Do you feel you walk in light with Him or does darkness sometimes enter your path? Focus this week on how He is the light of your world.

Stop...

Journal to the Lord about what this Promise means to you. Why is this promise important?

A

Ask...

Ask the Lord about how this Promise applies to your life right now. Speak from the heart about why you are asking.

L

Listen...

Lord, tell me what you have to say about how your Promise applies to me.

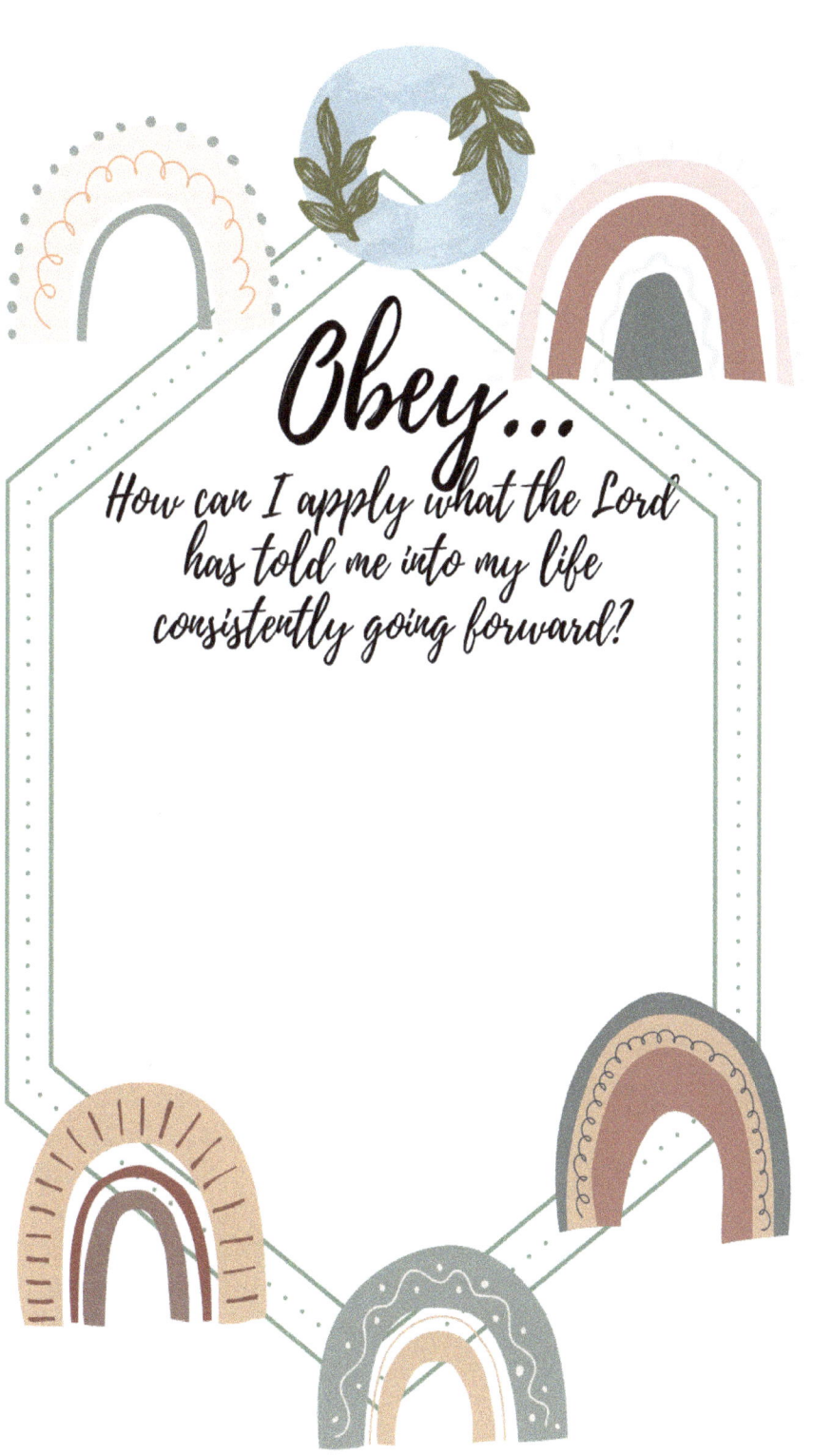

Obey...

How can I apply what the Lord has told me into my life consistently going forward?

So do not worry, saying, 'What shall we eat?' or 'What shall we drink?' or 'What shall we wear?' For the pagans run after all these things, and your heavenly Father knows that you need them. But seek first his kingdom and his righteousness, and all these things will be given to you as well.

Mt 6:31-33

Are you willing to seek the Lord for your needs? Will you let Him bear the burden or do you want to hold onto it and control it?

Stop...

Journal to the Lord about what this Promise means to you. Why is this promise important?

Ask...

Ask the Lord about how this Promise applies to your life right now. Speak from the heart about why you are asking.

L

Listen...

Lord, tell me what you have
to say about how your
Promise applies to me.

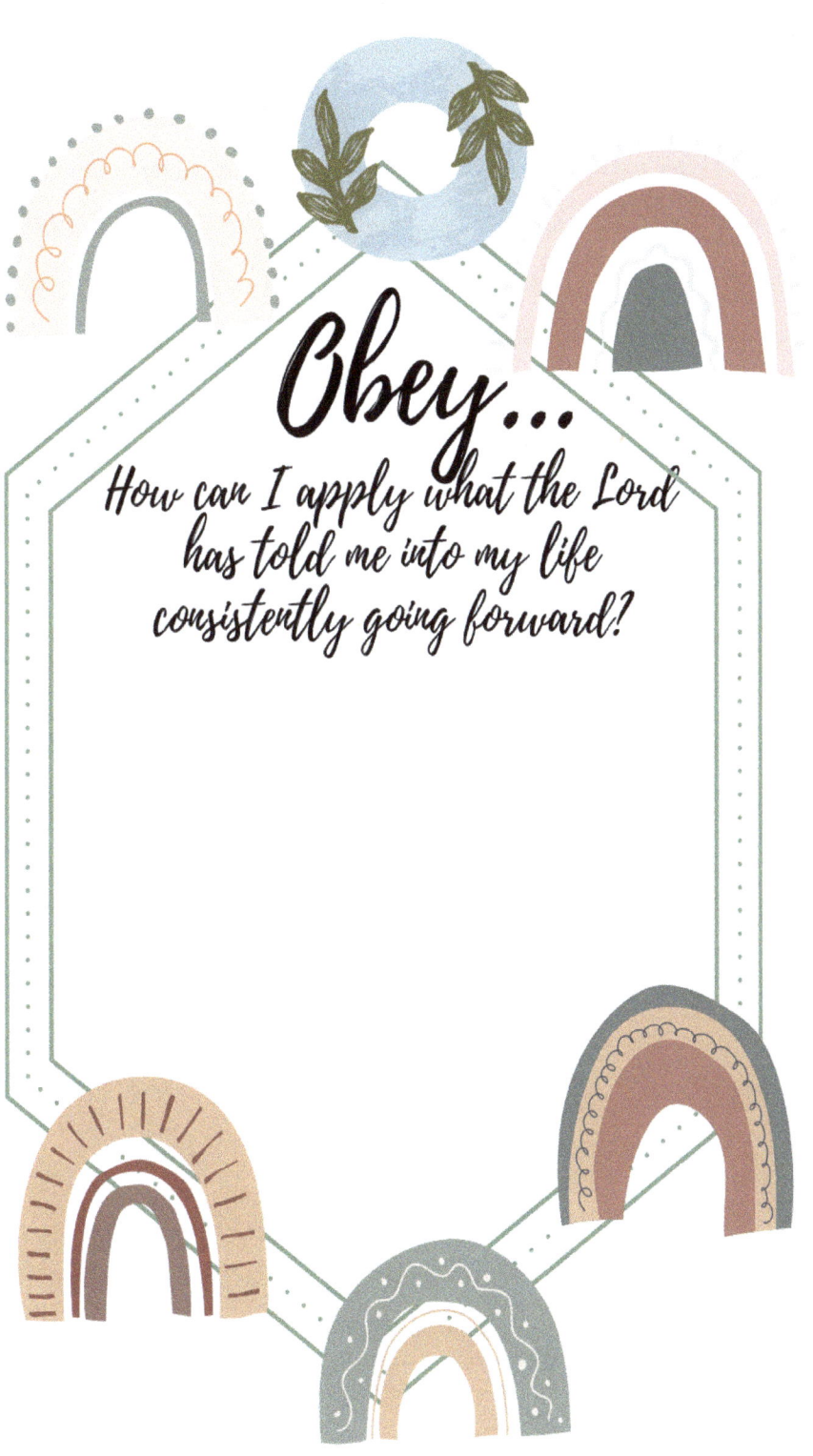

Obey...

How can I apply what the Lord has told me into my life consistently going forward?

Do not be anxious about anything, but in every situation, by prayer and petition, with thanksgiving, present your requests to God. And the peace of God, which transcends all understanding, will guard your hearts and your minds in Christ Jesus.

Phil 4:6-7

Do you spend time worrying before you present your requests to God? How can you redirect your focus to thanksgiving even in hard times?

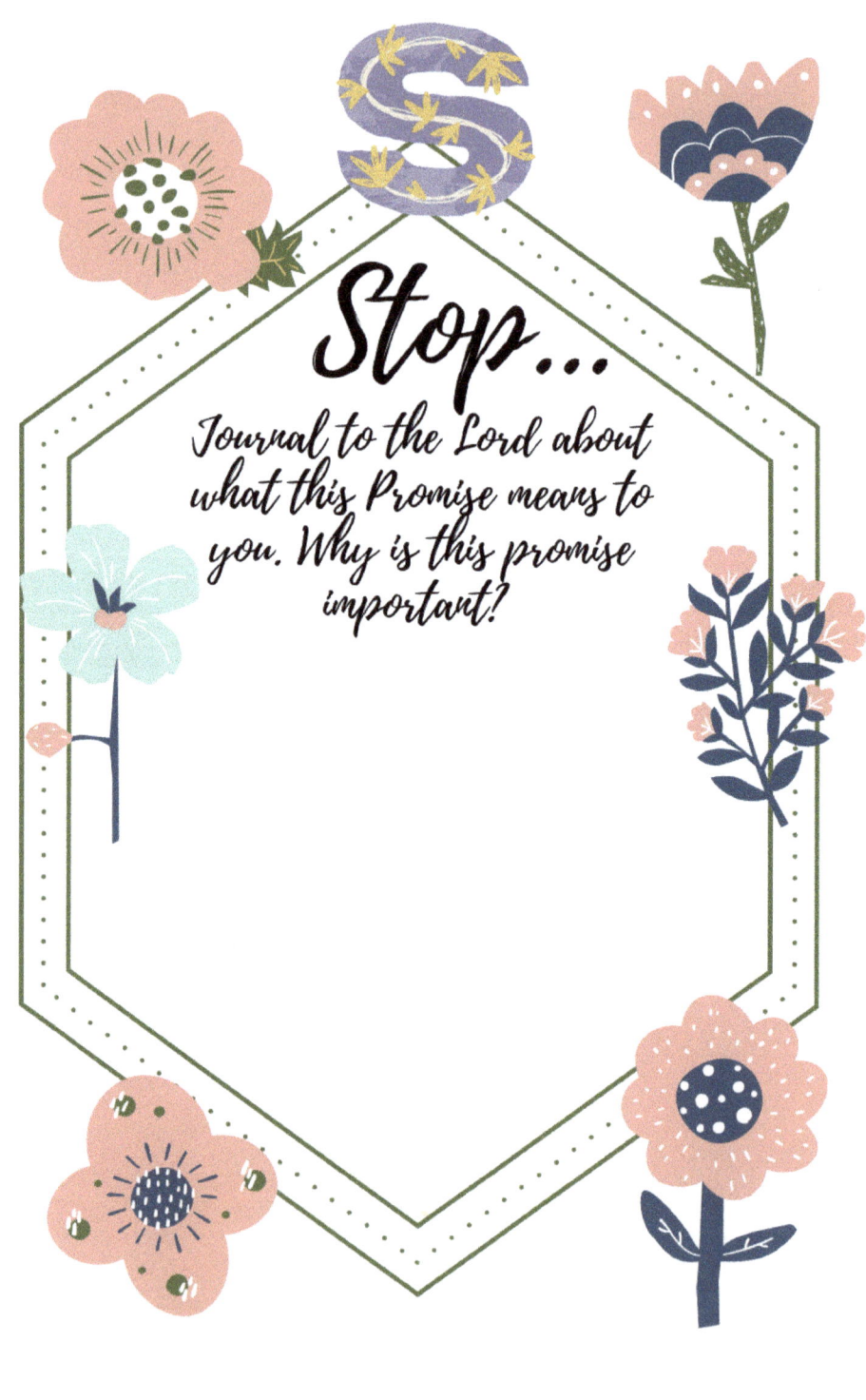

Stop...

Journal to the Lord about what this Promise means to you. Why is this promise important?

A

Ask...

Ask the Lord about how this Promise applies to your life right now. Speak from the heart about why you are asking.

L

Listen...

Lord, tell me what you have to say about how your Promise applies to me.

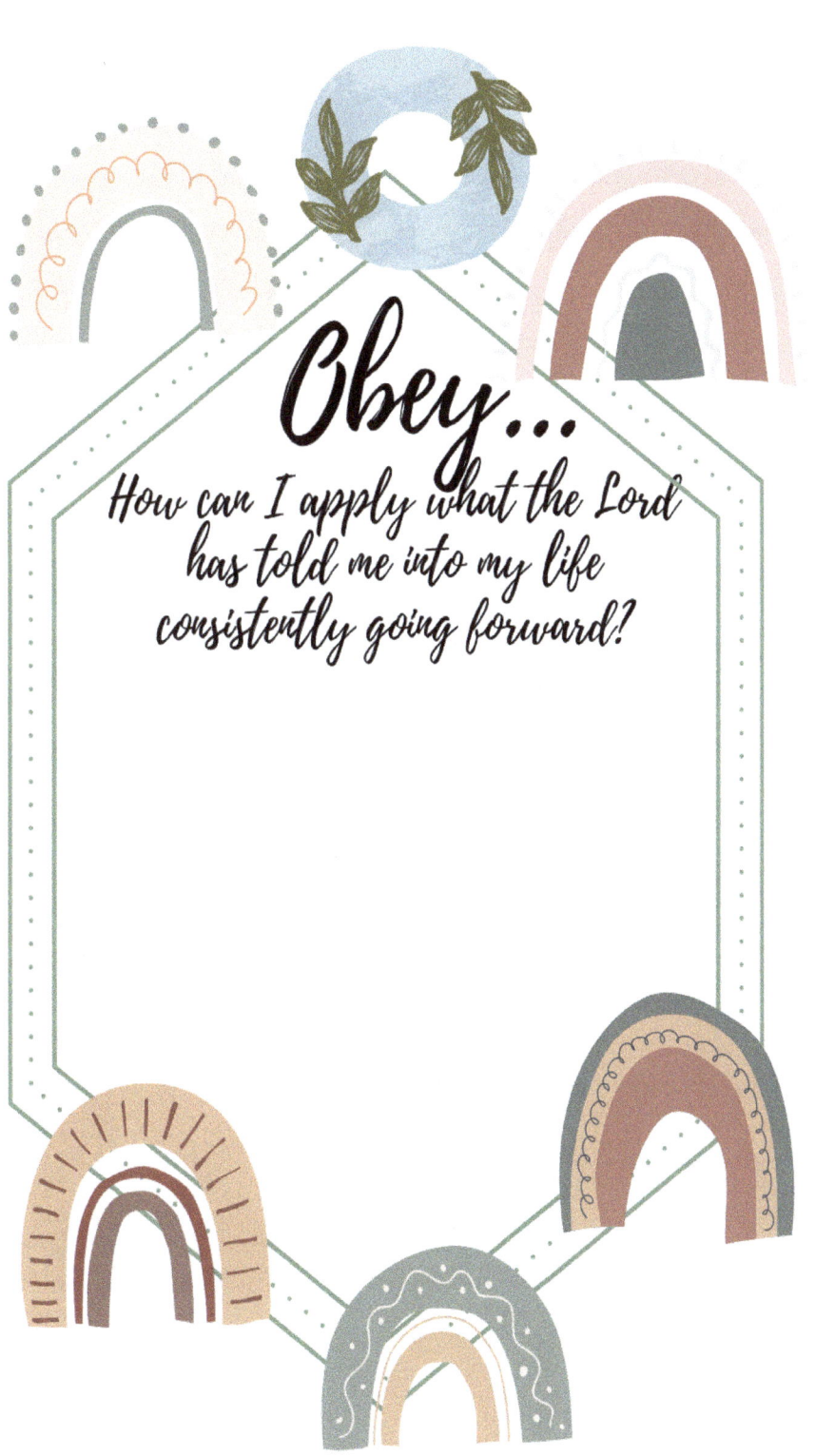

Obey...

How can I apply what the Lord has told me into my life consistently going forward?

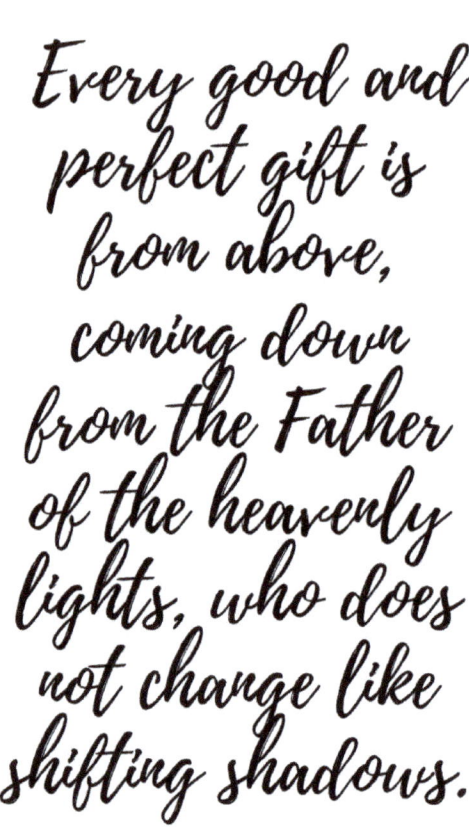

Every good and
perfect gift is
from above,
coming down
from the Father
of the heavenly
lights, who does
not change like
shifting shadows.

James 1:17

Do you believe that what God gives you are good and perfect gifts? Do you now in your heart He is the same yesterday, today and tomorrow?

Stop...

Journal to the Lord about what this Promise means to you. Why is this promise important?

Ask...

Ask the Lord about how this Promise applies to your life right now. Speak from the heart about why you are asking.

Listen...

Lord, tell me what you have to say about how your Promise applies to me.

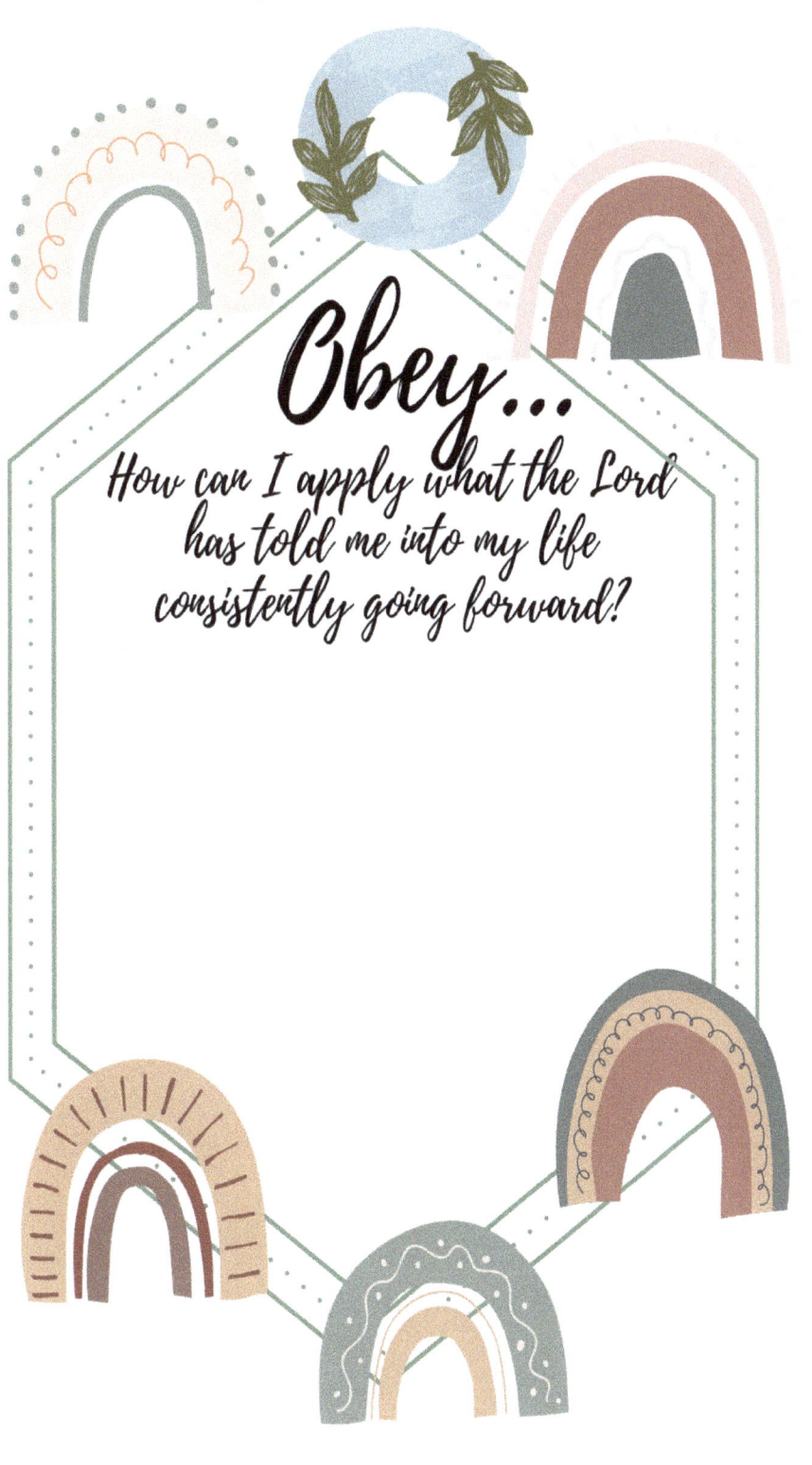

Obey...

How can I apply what the Lord has told me into my life consistently going forward?

Sovereign Lord, you are God! Your covenant is trustworthy, and you have promised these good things to your servant. . .

2 Sam 7:28

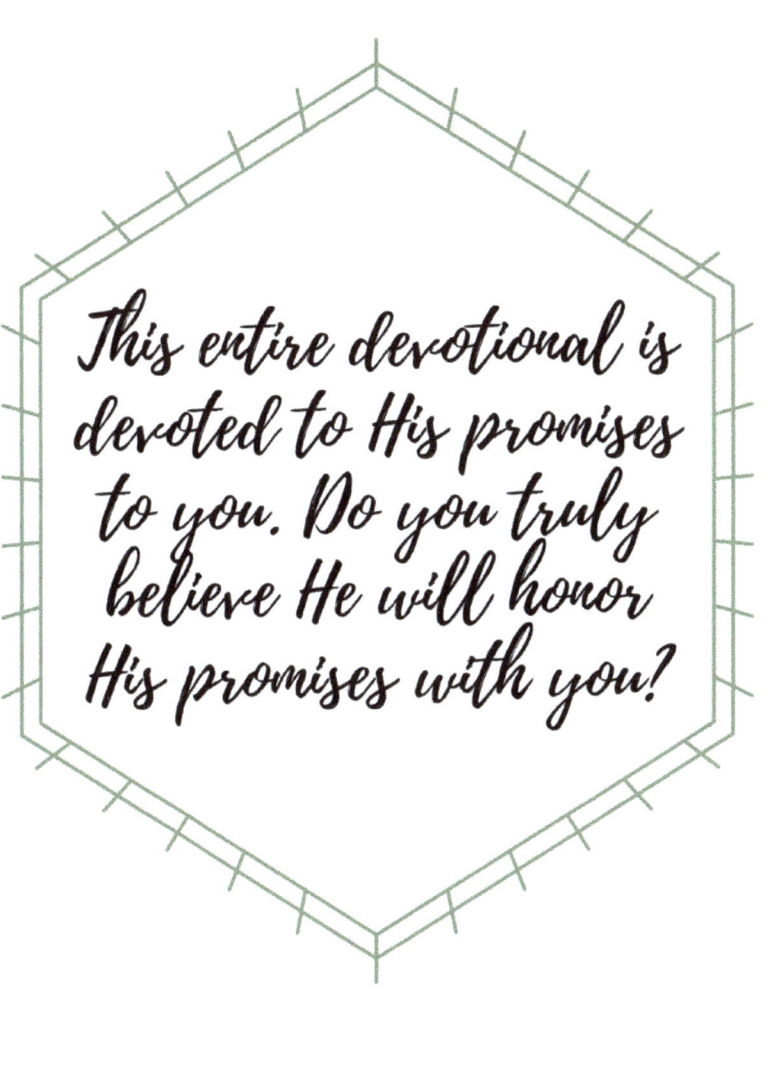

This entire devotional is devoted to His promises to you. Do you truly believe He will honor His promises with you?

Stop...

Journal to the Lord about what this Promise means to you. Why is this promise important?

Ask...

Ask the Lord about how this Promise applies to your life right now. Speak from the heart about why you are asking.

Listen...

Lord, tell me what you have to say about how your Promise applies to me.

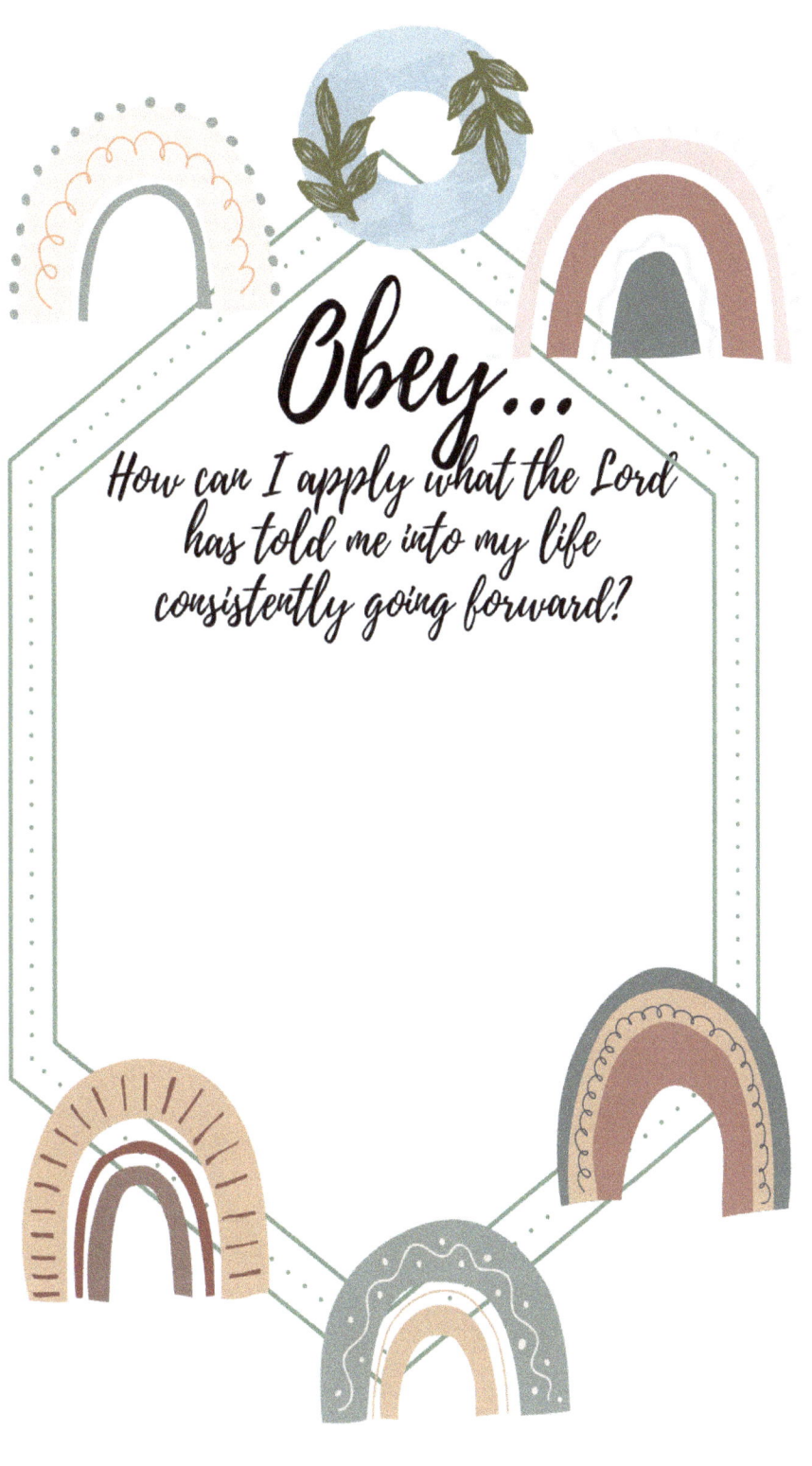

Obey...

How can I apply what the Lord has told me into my life consistently going forward?

The Lord is good, a refuge in times of trouble. He cares for those who trust in him.

Nahum 1:7

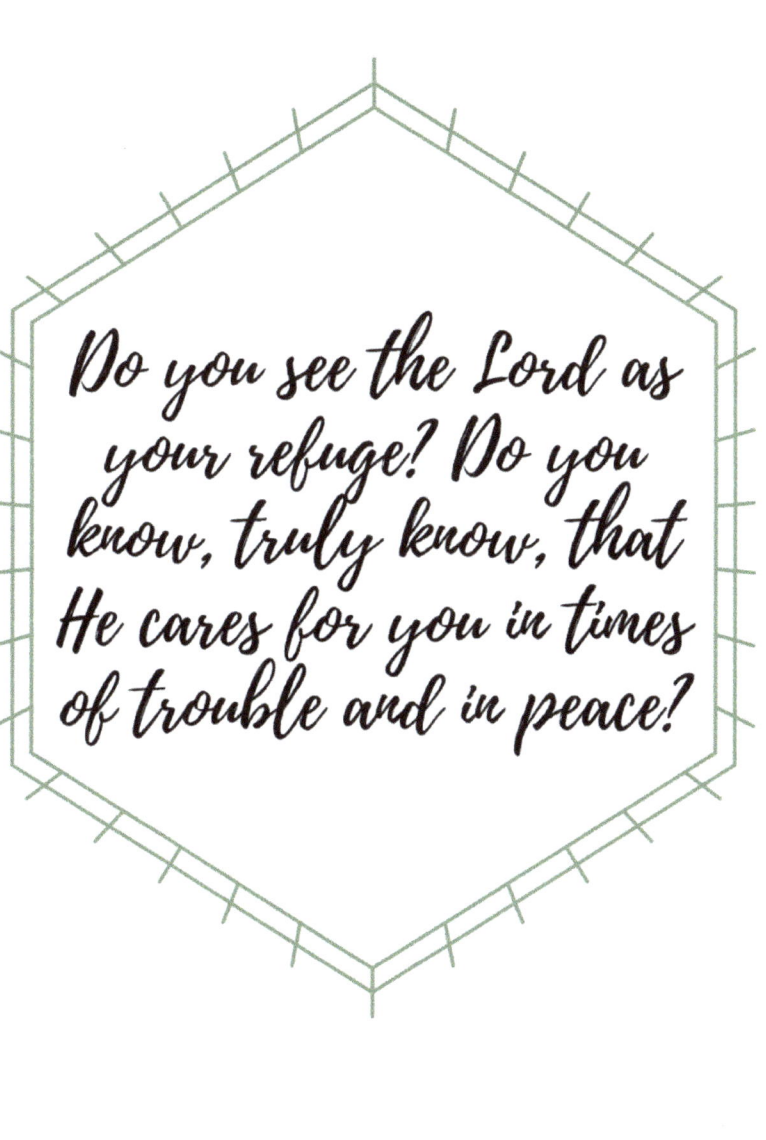

Do you see the Lord as your refuge? Do you know, truly know, that He cares for you in times of trouble and in peace?

Stop...

Journal to the Lord about what this Promise means to you. Why is this promise important?

Ask...

Ask the Lord about how this Promise applies to your life right now. Speak from the heart about why you are asking.

L

Listen...

Lord, tell me what you have
to say about how your
Promise applies to me.

Obey...

How can I apply what the Lord has told me into my life consistently going forward?

Have I not commanded you? Be strong and courageous. Do not be afraid; do not be discouraged, for the Lord your God will be with you wherever you go.

Joshua 1:9

Do you feel the Lord with you wherever you go? Is there anything holding you back from feeling strong and courageous. Speak to the Lord about that.

Stop...

Journal to the Lord about what this Promise means to you. Why is this promise important?

A

Ask...

Ask the Lord about how this Promise applies to your life right now. Speak from the heart about why you are asking.

L

Listen...

Lord, tell me what you have to say about how your Promise applies to me.

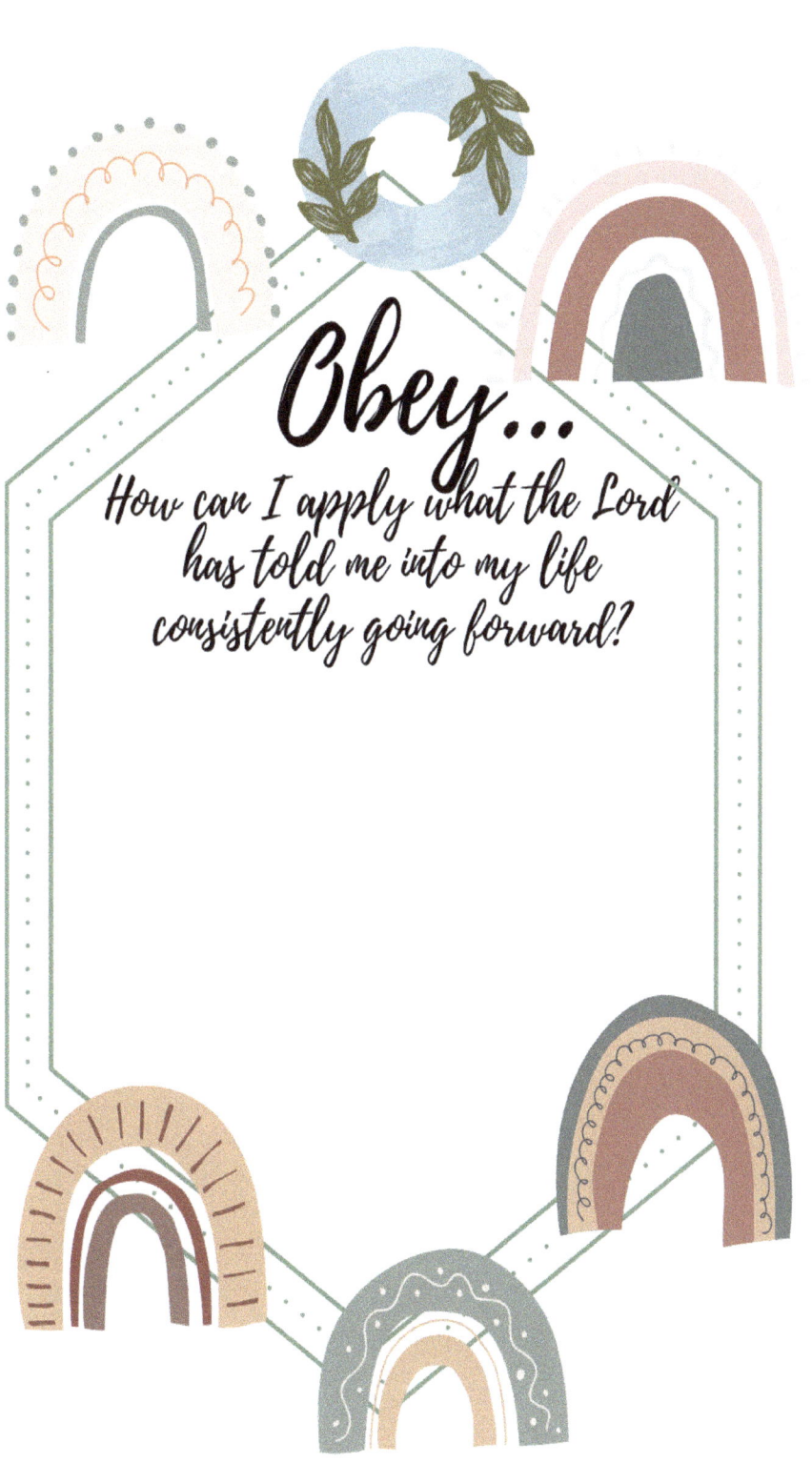

Obey...

How can I apply what the Lord has told me into my life consistently going forward?

Yes, I am the vine; you are the branches. Those who remain in me, and I in them, will produce much fruit. For apart from me you can do nothing.

John 15:5

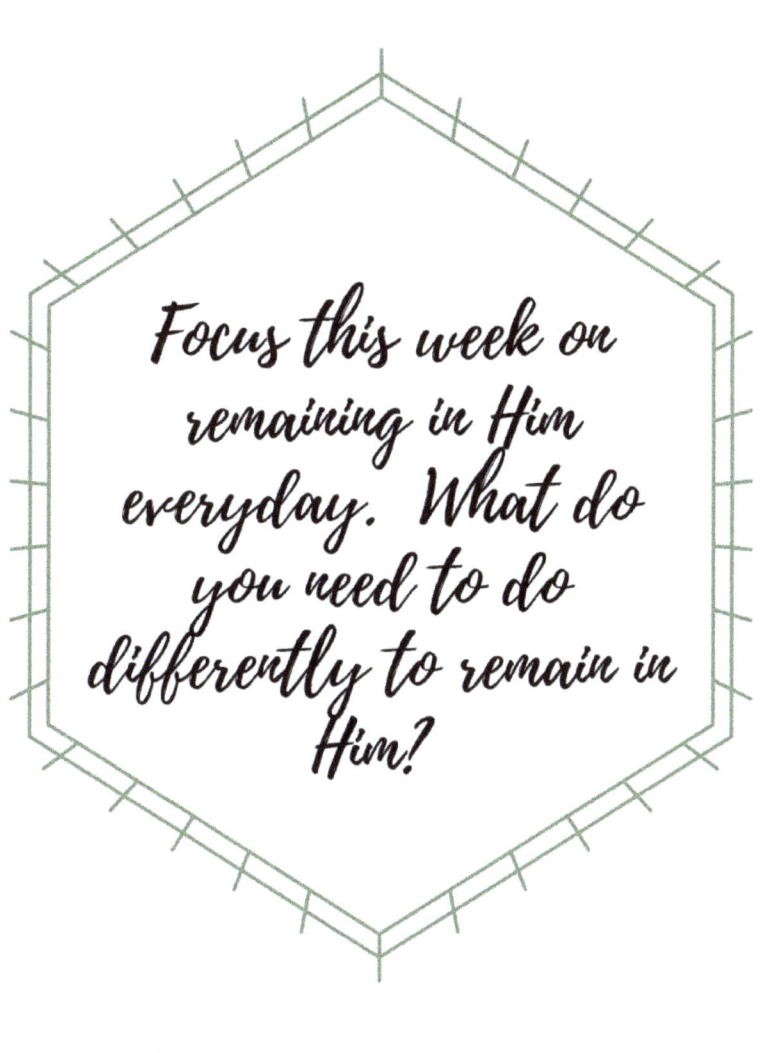

Focus this week on remaining in Him everyday. What do you need to do differently to remain in Him?

Stop...

Journal to the Lord about what this Promise means to you. Why is this promise important?

A

Ask...

Ask the Lord about how this Promise applies to your life right now. Speak from the heart about why you are asking.

Listen...

Lord, tell me what you have to say about how your Promise applies to me.

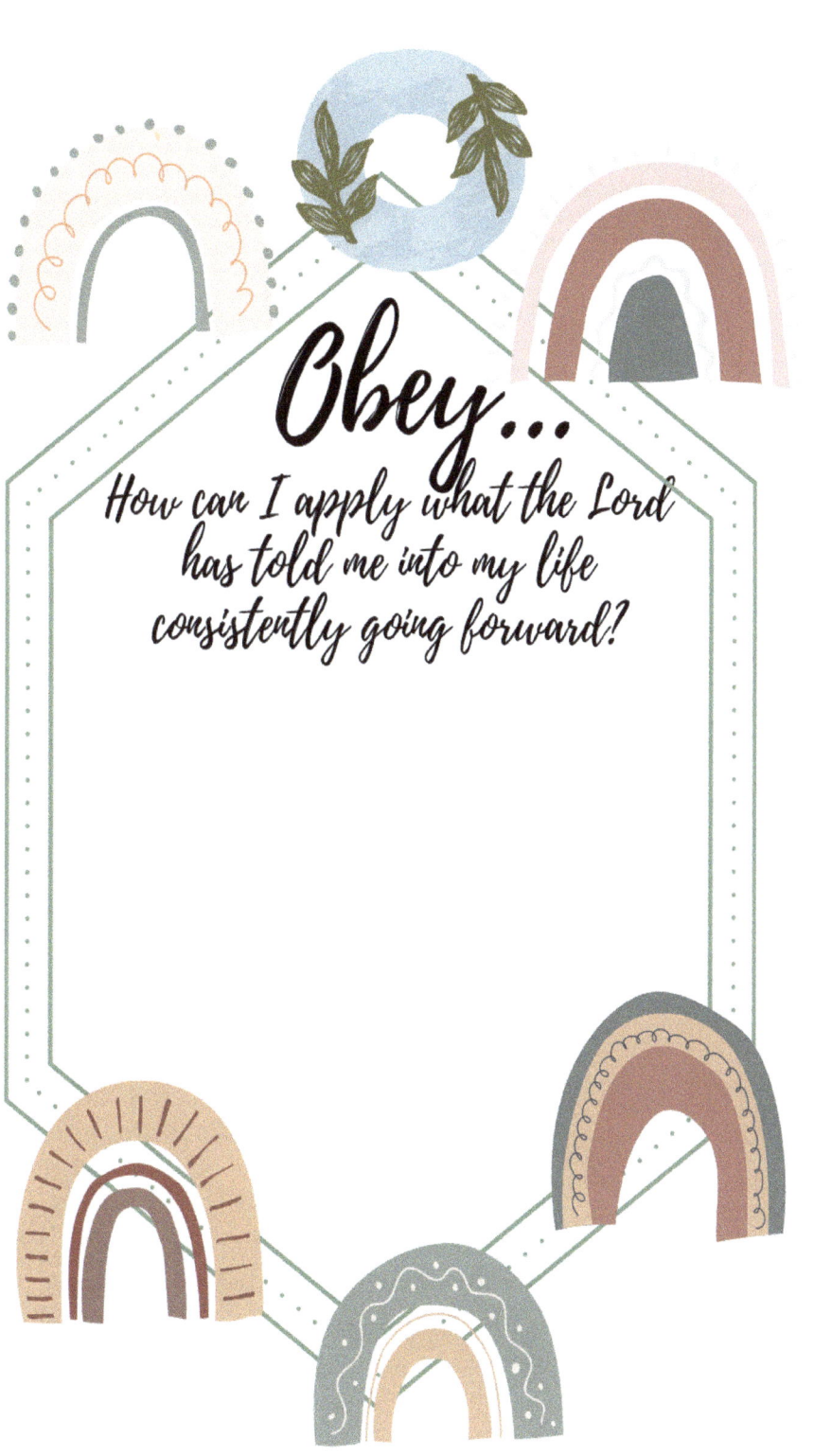

Obey...

How can I apply what the Lord has told me into my life consistently going forward?

Blessed is the one
who does not walk in step
with the wicked
or stand in the way that sinners
take
or sit in the company of
mockers,
but whose delight is in the law
of the Lord,
and who meditates on his law
day and night.
That person is like a tree
planted by streams of water,
which yields its fruit in
season
and whose leaf does not wither
—
whatever they do prospers.

Psalm 1:1-3

What areas do you need to change to not walk in step with the wicked but to instead delight in the Lord? Are you yielding good fruit?

S

Stop...

Journal to the Lord about what this Promise means to you. Why is this promise important?

A

Ask...

Ask the Lord about how this Promise applies to your life right now. Speak from the heart about why you are asking.

L

Listen...

Lord, tell me what you have to say about how your Promise applies to me.

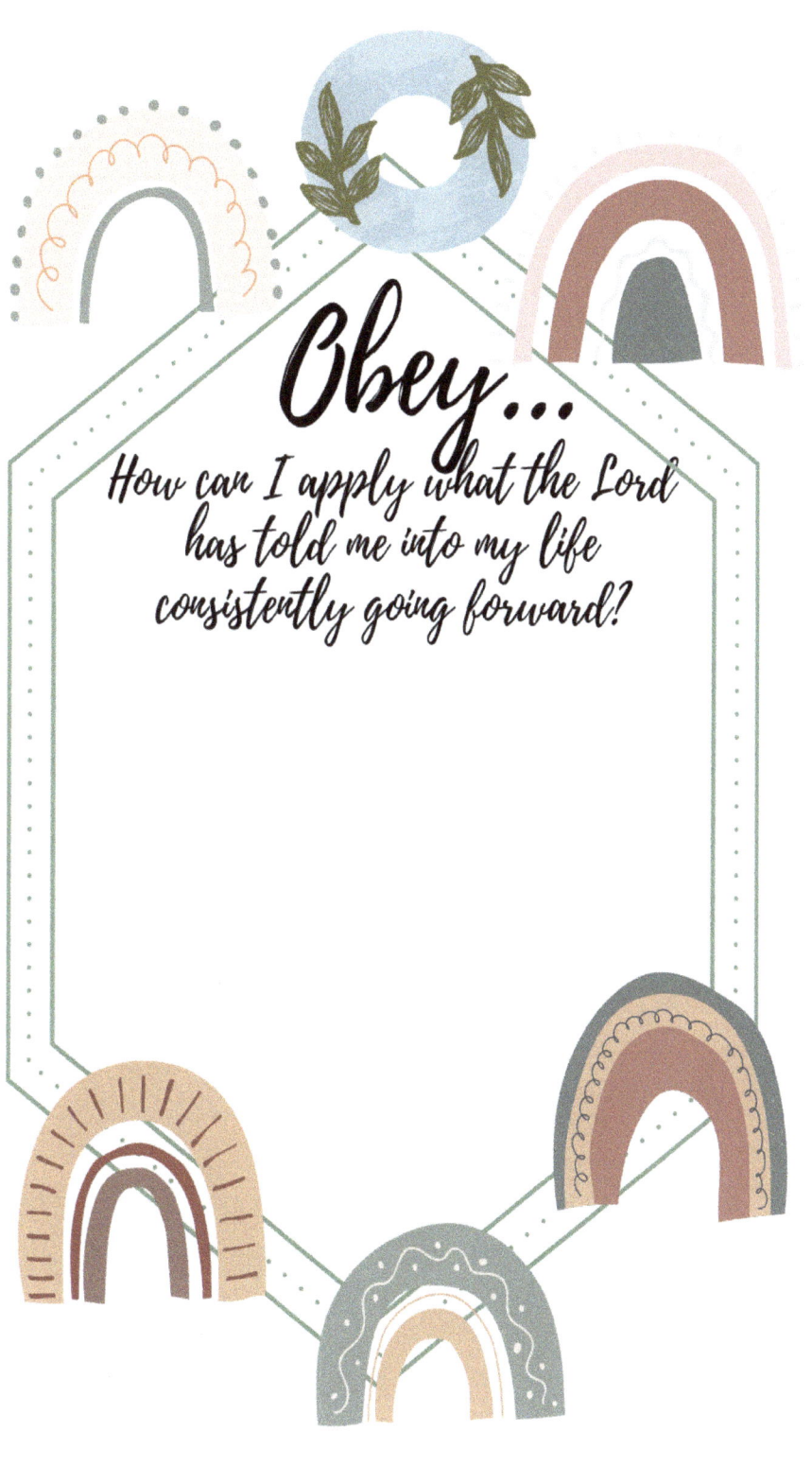

Obey...

How can I apply what the Lord has told me into my life consistently going forward?

The Lord will fight for you; you need only to be still.

Exodus 14:14

When you are in times of trouble are you able to be still and let the Lord fight your battles? Do you try to fight in your own will your own way?

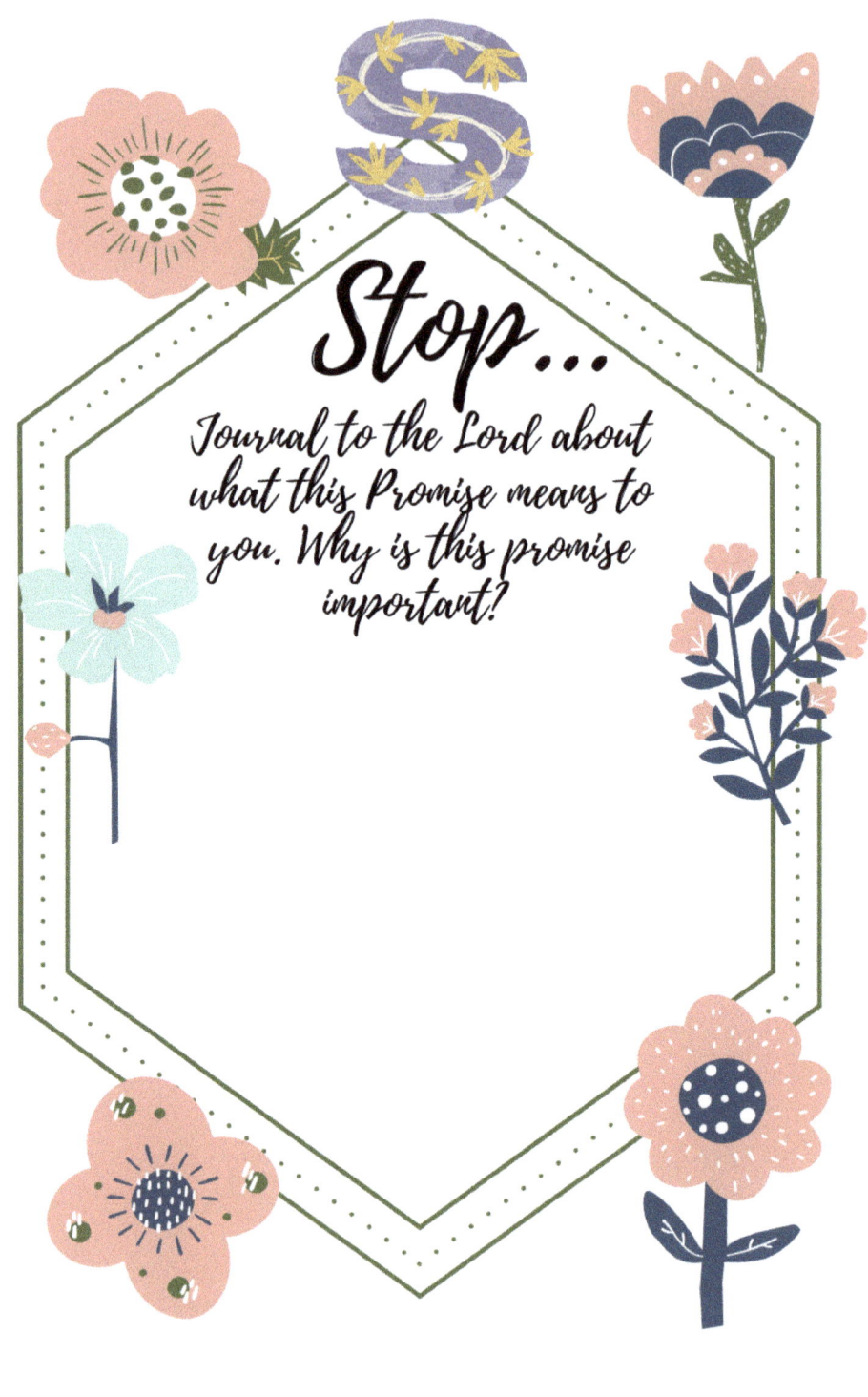

Stop...

Journal to the Lord about what this Promise means to you. Why is this promise important?

A

Ask...

Ask the Lord about how this Promise applies to your life right now. Speak from the heart about why you are asking.

Listen...

Lord, tell me what you have to say about how your Promise applies to me.

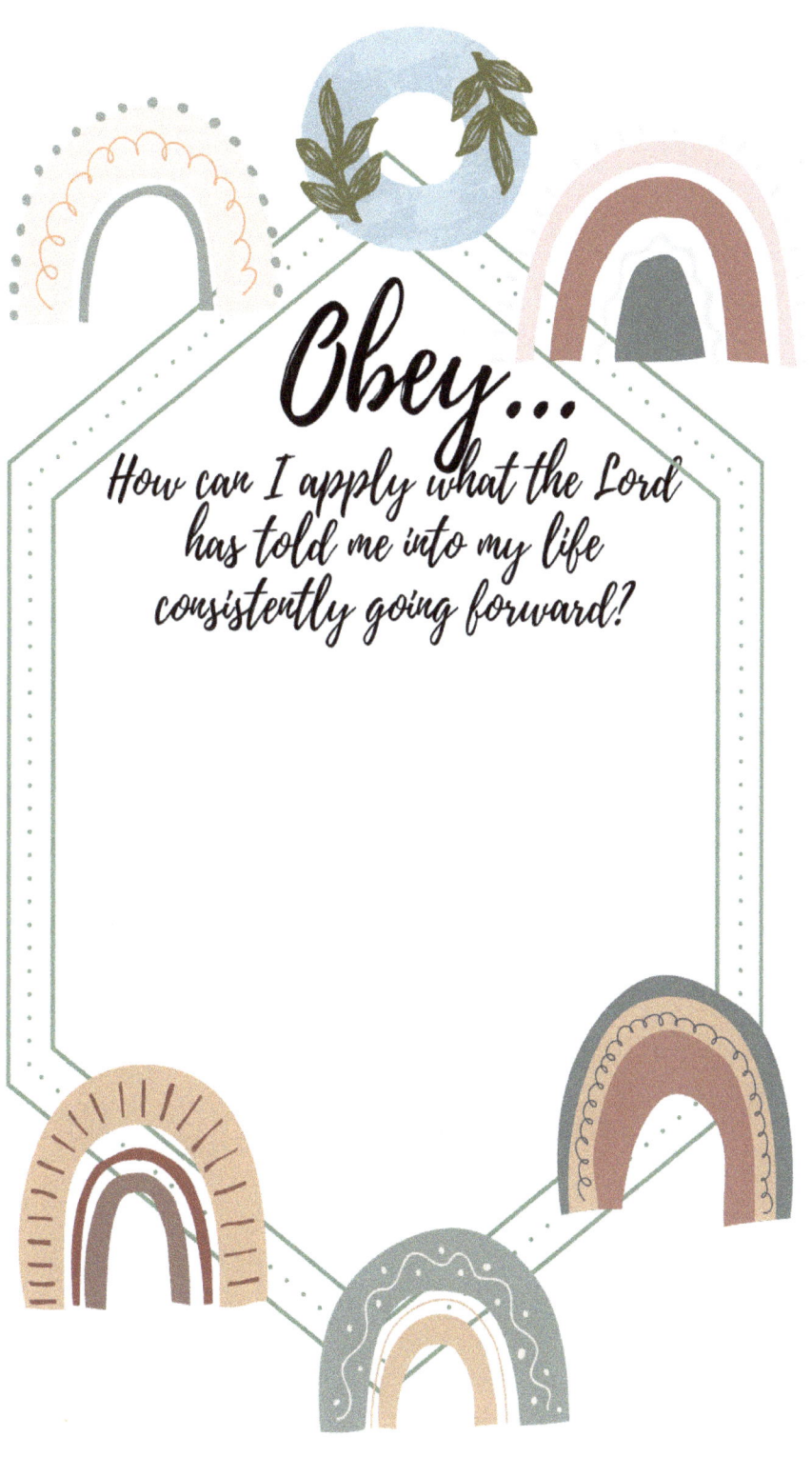

Obey...

How can I apply what the Lord has told me into my life consistently going forward?

no weapon forged
against you will
prevail,
and you will
refute every tongue
that accuses you.
This is the heritage
of the servants of
the Lord,
and this is their
vindication from me,"
declares the Lord.

Isaiah 54:17

Think this week about weapons that have been directed at you and accusations made against you. Did you seek God in those times? How did He prevail on your behalf?

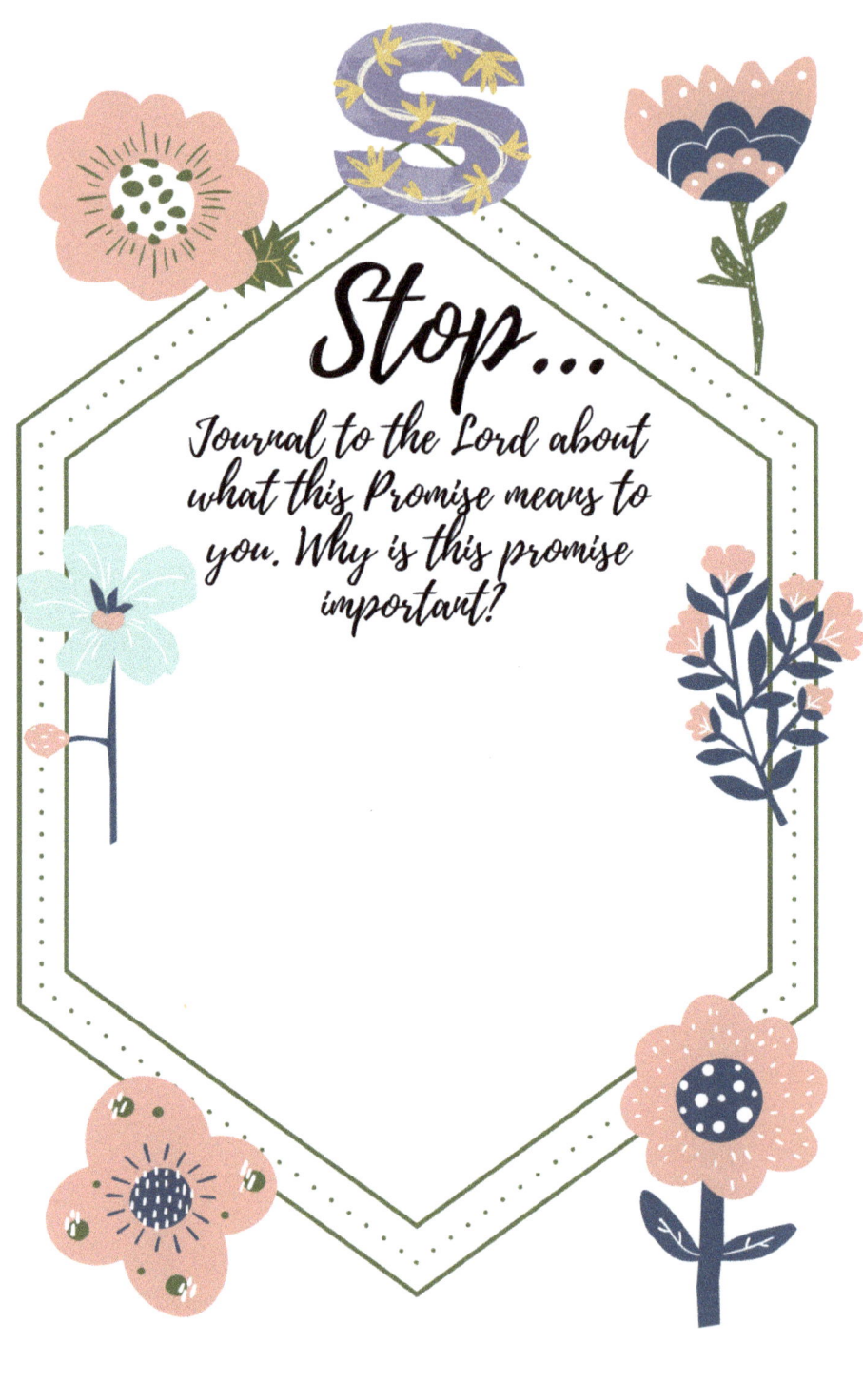

Stop...

Journal to the Lord about what this Promise means to you. Why is this promise important?

A

Ask...

Ask the Lord about how this Promise applies to your life right now. Speak from the heart about why you are asking.

Listen...

Lord, tell me what you have
to say about how your
Promise applies to me.

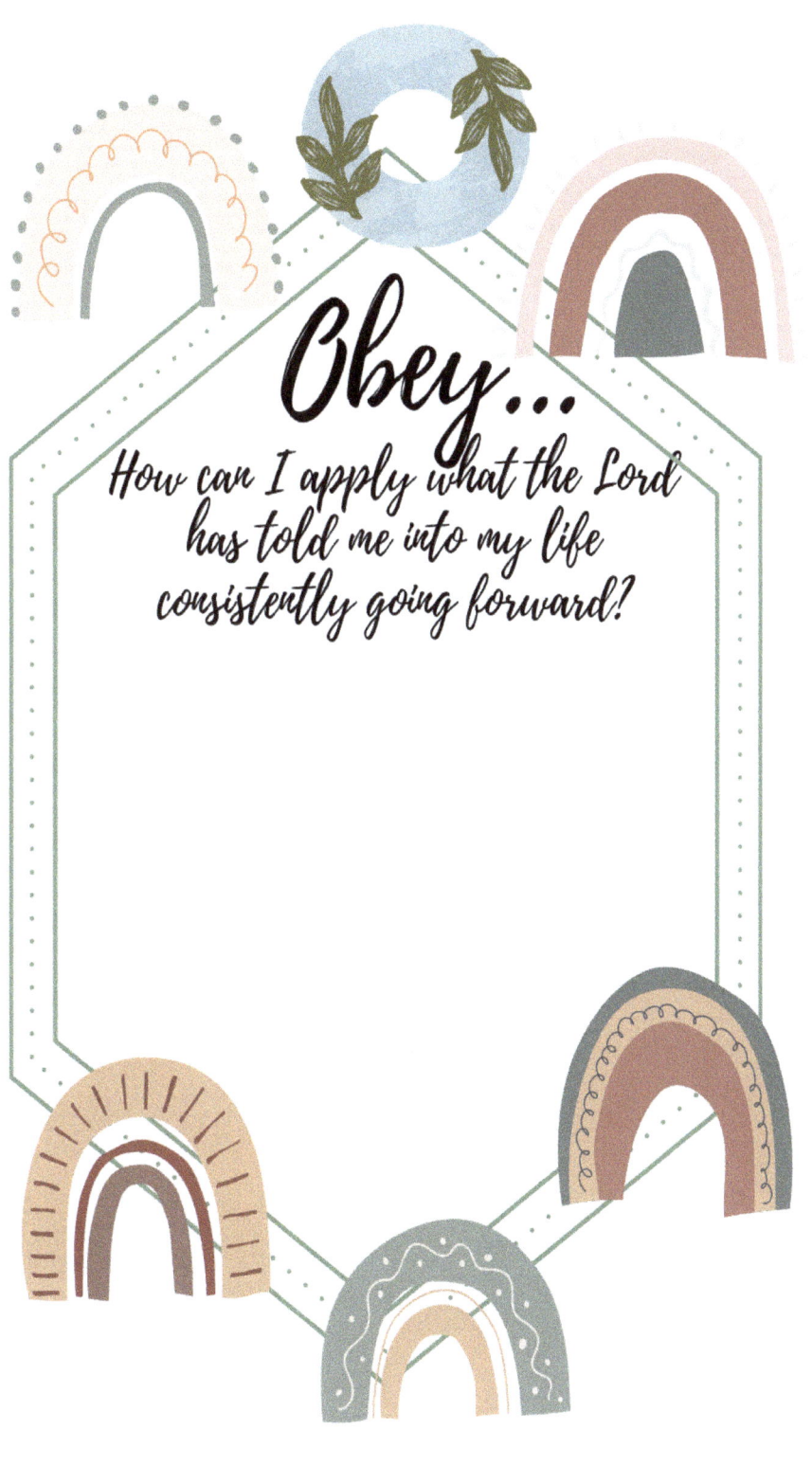

Obey...

How can I apply what the Lord has told me into my life consistently going forward?

Submit yourselves, then, to God. Resist the devil, and he will flee from you.

James 4:7

Are there any areas of your life you are resistant to submit to God? Are you quick to flee the enemy when he is near you?

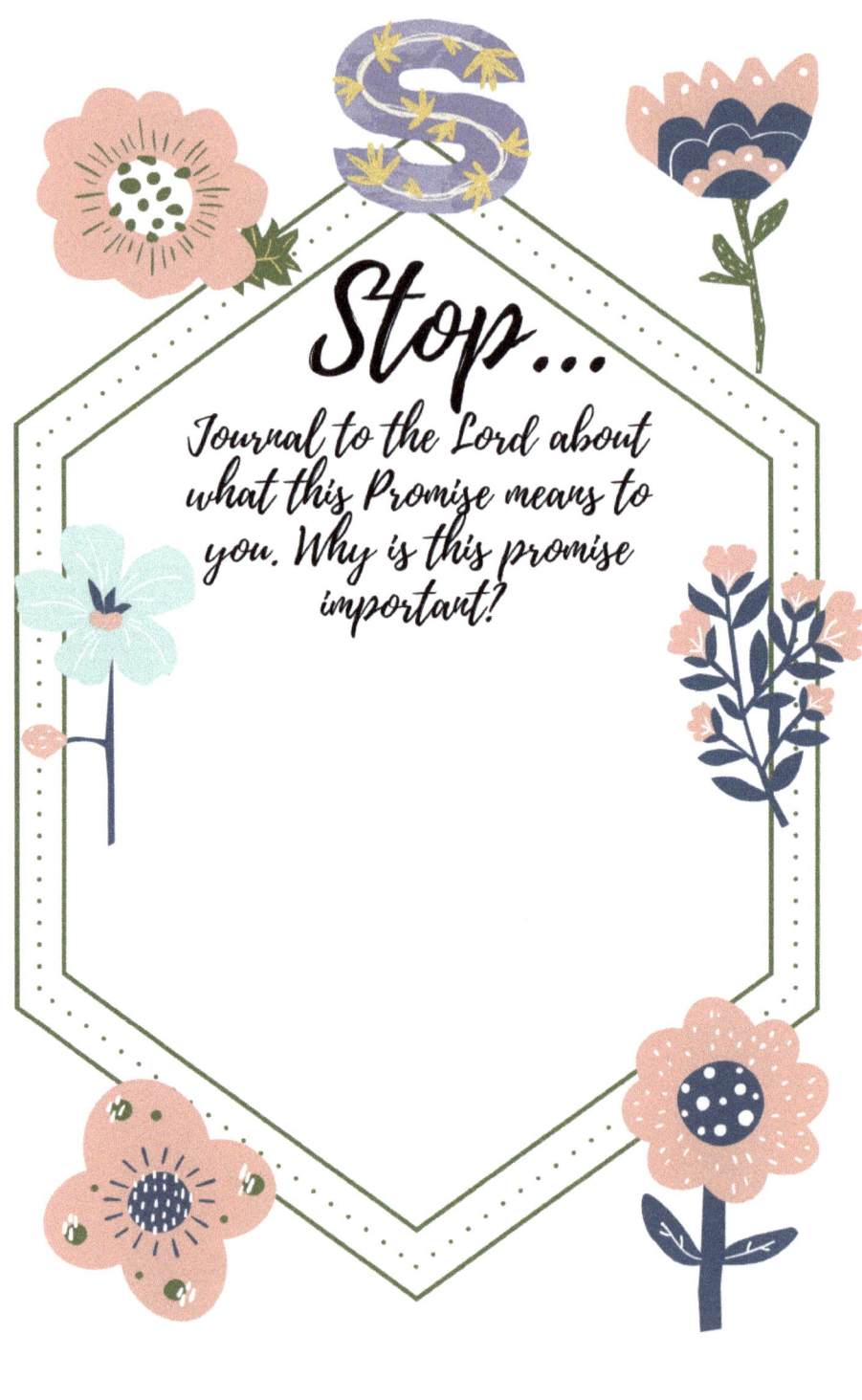

Stop...

Journal to the Lord about what this Promise means to you. Why is this promise important?

Ask...

Ask the Lord about how this Promise applies to your life right now. Speak from the heart about why you are asking.

Listen...

Lord, tell me what you have to say about how your Promise applies to me.

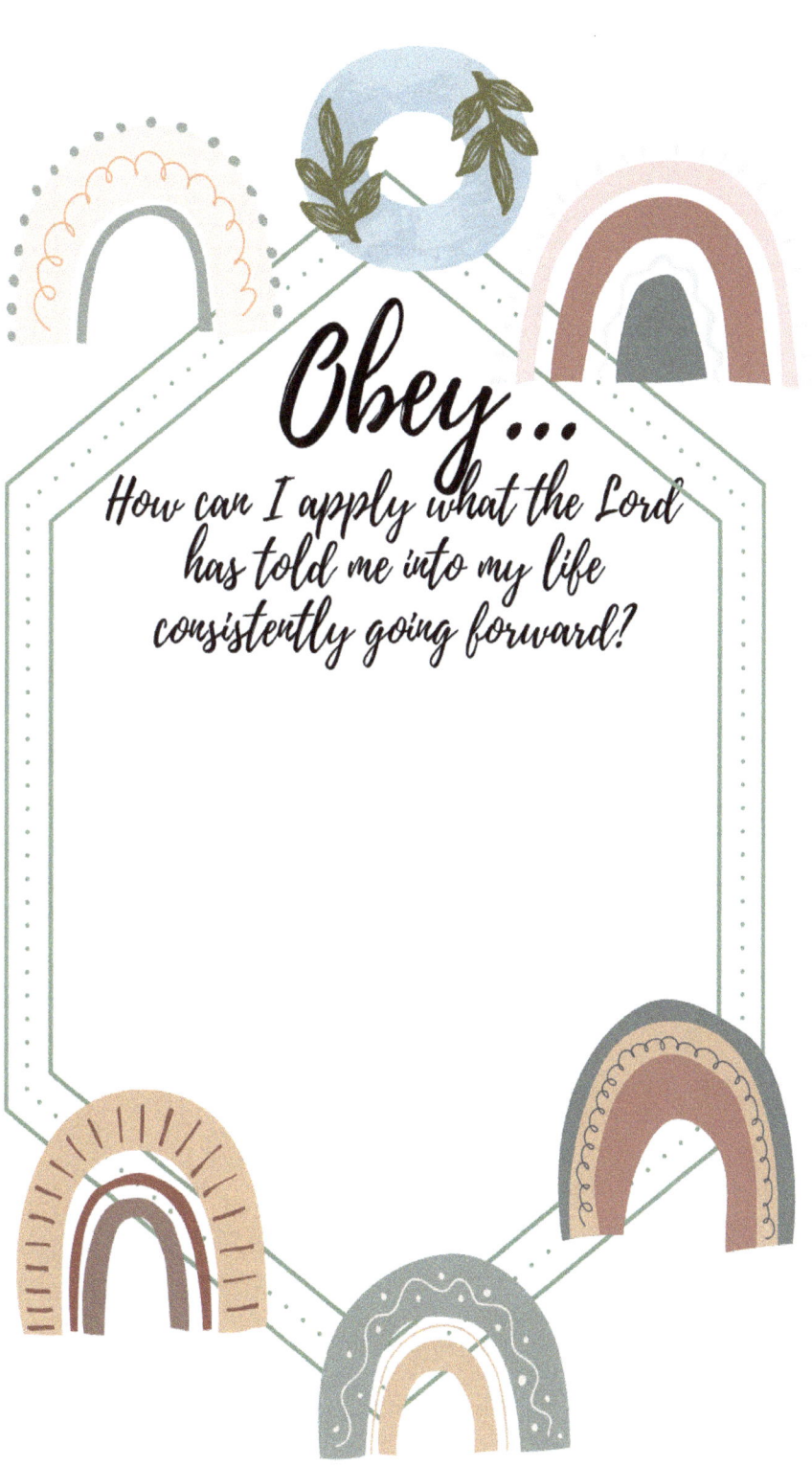

Obey...

How can I apply what the Lord
has told me into my life
consistently going forward?

Bring the whole tithe into the storehouse, that there may be food in my house. Test me in this," says the Lord Almighty, "and see if I will not throw open the floodgates of heaven and pour out so much blessing that there will not be room enough to store it.

Malachi 3:10

Do you trust the Lord with all that you have? Focus this week on how you can show the Lord your willingness to trust Him in all things.

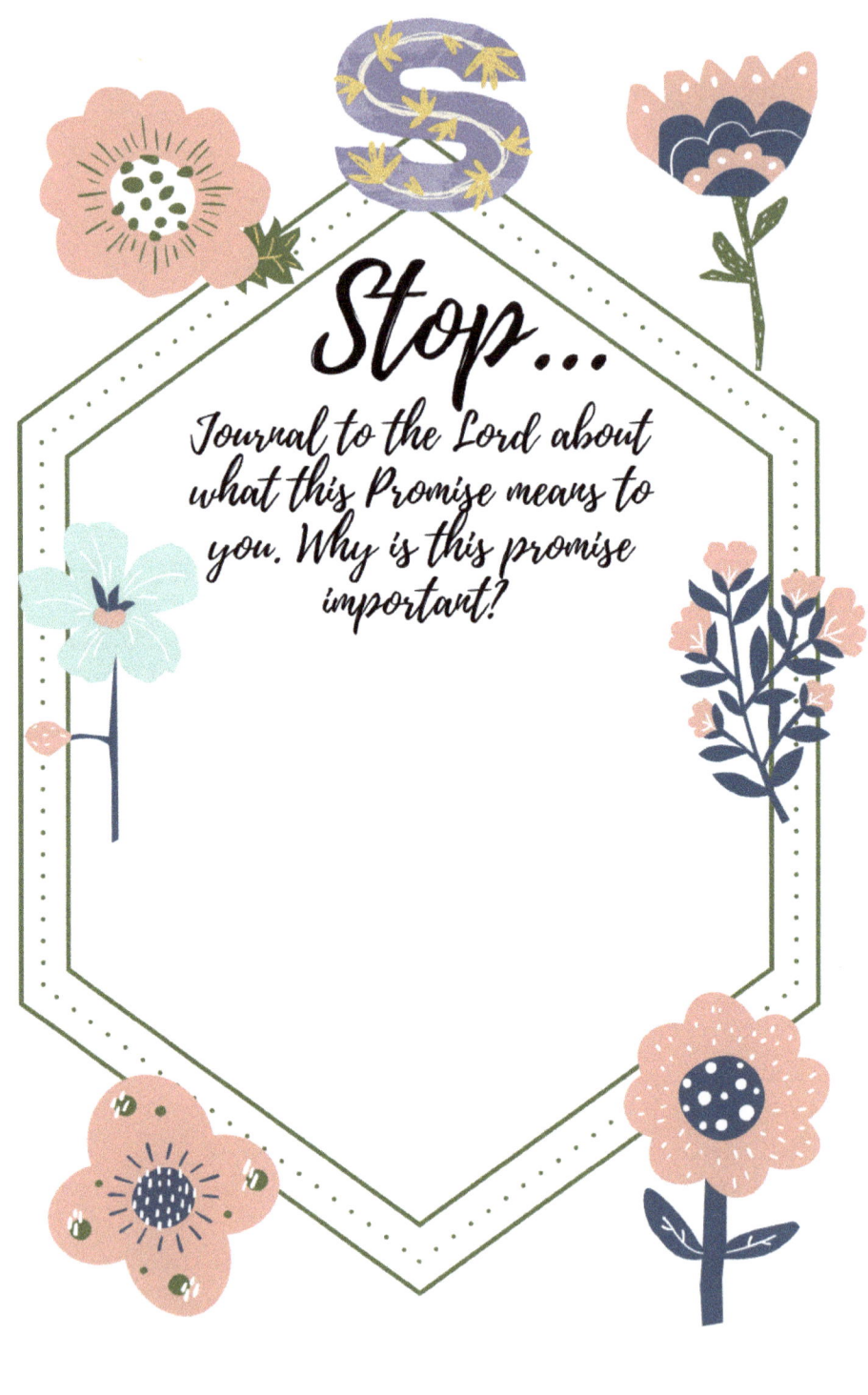

Stop...

Journal to the Lord about what this Promise means to you. Why is this promise important?

A

Ask...

Ask the Lord about how this Promise applies to your life right now. Speak from the heart about why you are asking.

L

Listen...

Lord, tell me what you have
to say about how your
Promise applies to me.

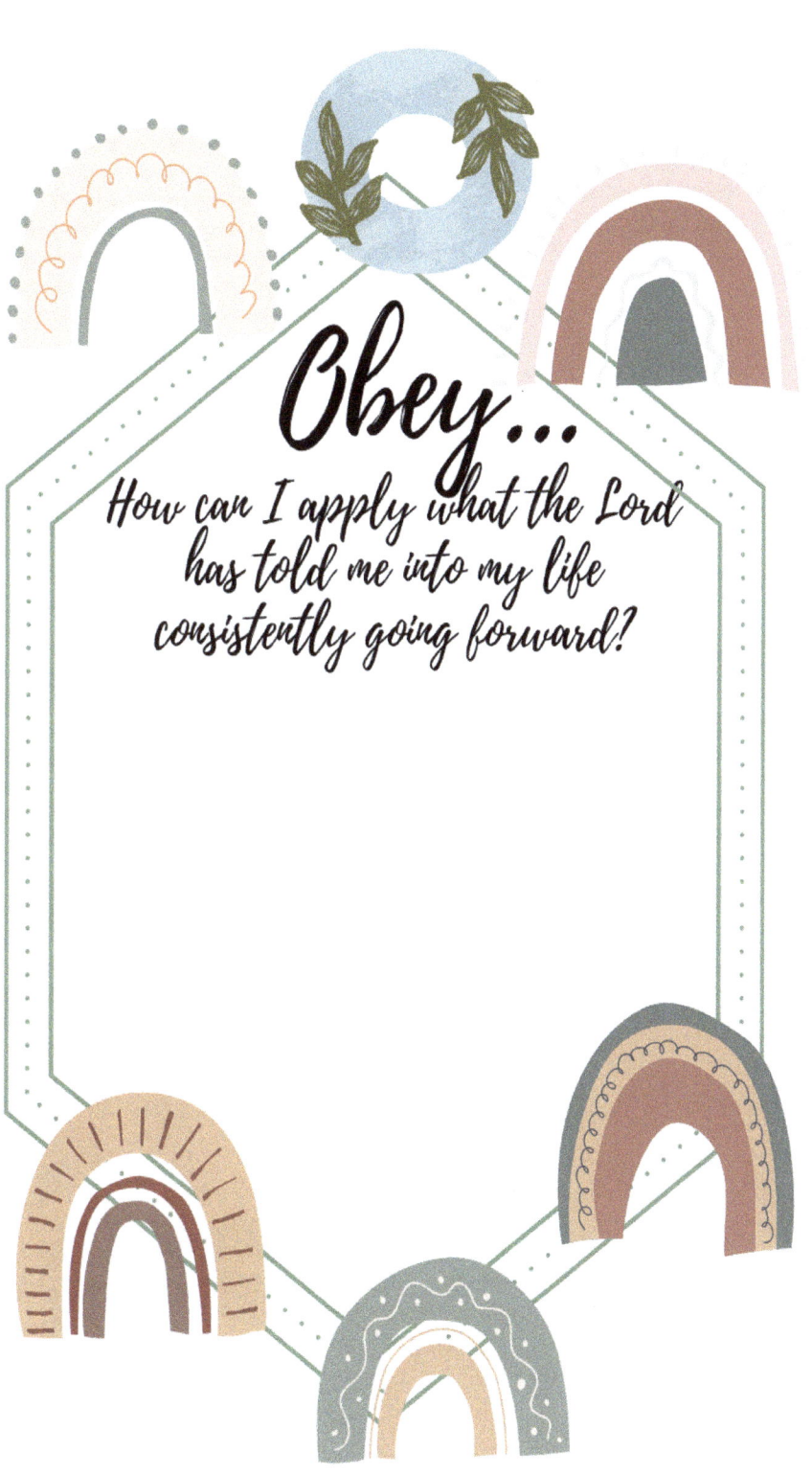

Obey...

How can I apply what the Lord has told me into my life consistently going forward?

I thank my God every time I remember you. In all my prayers for all of you, I always pray with joy because of your partnership in the gospel from the first day until now, being confident of this, that he who began a good work in you will carry it on to completion until the day of Christ Jesus.

Phil 1:3-6

Think about the good work the Lord has done in your life. How do you feel knowing He will continue to work in you until you meet Him in heaven?

Stop...

Journal to the Lord about what this Promise means to you. Why is this promise important?

Ask...

Ask the Lord about how this Promise applies to your life right now. Speak from the heart about why you are asking.

Listen...

Lord, tell me what you have
to say about how your
Promise applies to me.

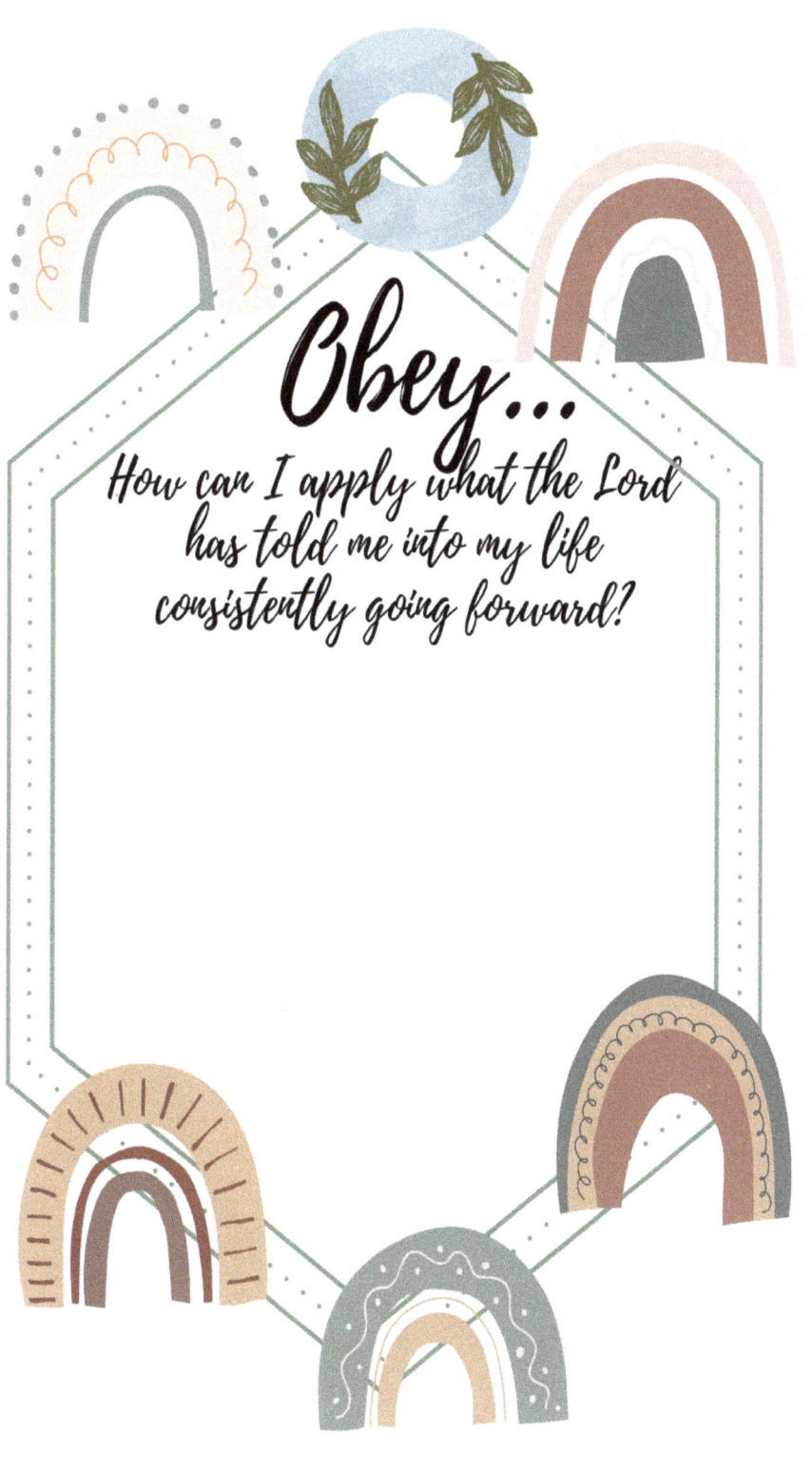

Obey...

How can I apply what the Lord has told me into my life consistently going forward?

"I have told you these things, so that in me you may have peace. In this world you will have trouble. But take heart! I have overcome the world."

John 16:33

Does knowing that the Jesus has overcome the world bring you peace? How do you feel that peace daily when you are dealing with the trouble of the world?

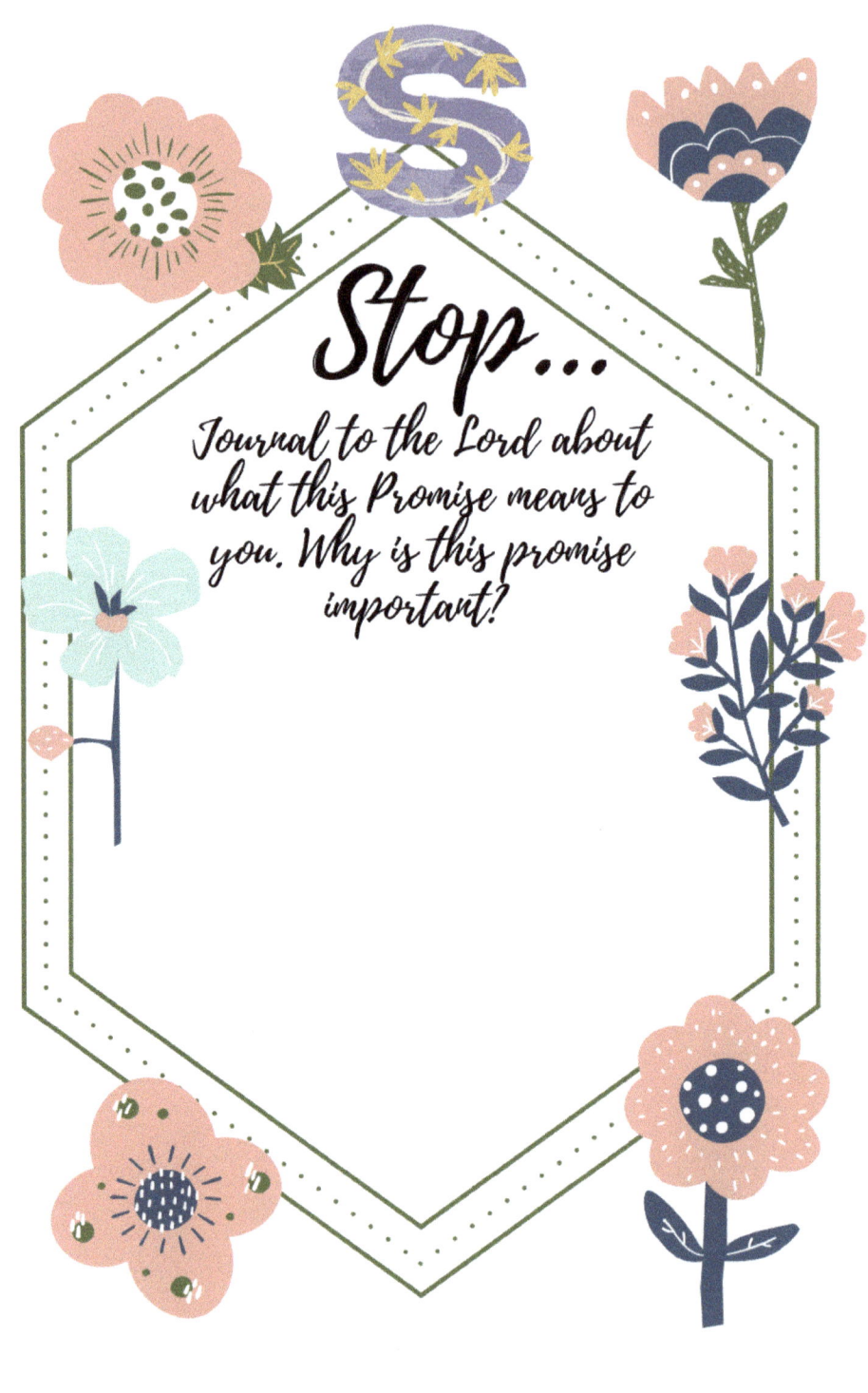

Stop...

Journal to the Lord about what this Promise means to you. Why is this promise important?

A

Ask...

Ask the Lord about how this Promise applies to your life right now. Speak from the heart about why you are asking.

L

Listen...

Lord, tell me what you have
to say about how your
Promise applies to me.

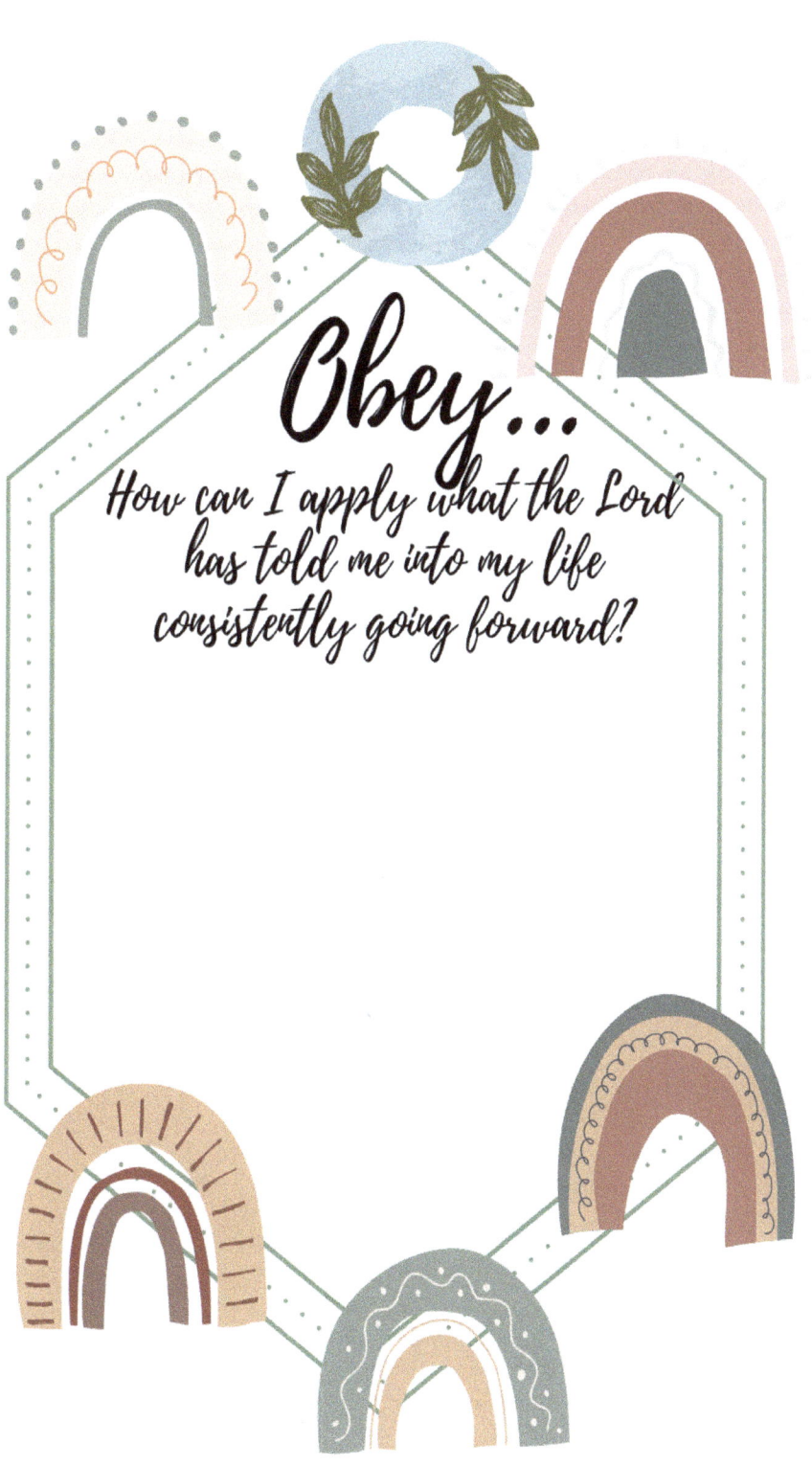

Obey...

How can I apply what the Lord
has told me into my life
consistently going forward?

Give thanks to the Lord, for he is good; his love endures forever.

1 Chronicles 16:34

Focus this week on giving thanks to the Lord. Thank Him for His enduring love for you

Stop...

Journal to the Lord about what this Promise means to you. Why is this promise important?

Ask...

Ask the Lord about how this Promise applies to your life right now. Speak from the heart about why you are asking.

Listen...

Lord, tell me what you have to say about how your Promise applies to me.

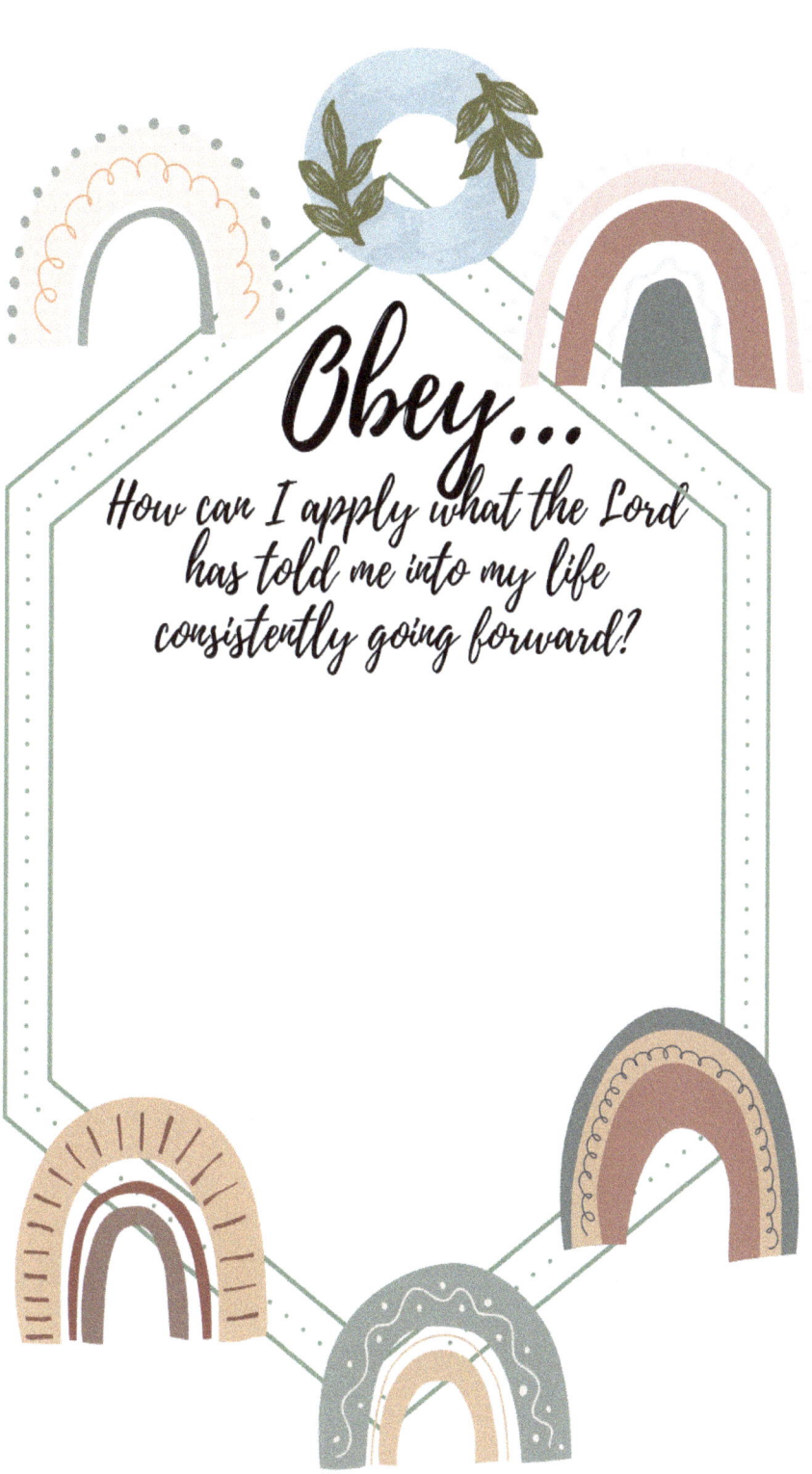

Obey...

How can I apply what the Lord has told me into my life consistently going forward?

ABOUT THE AUTHOR

Dawn is an author and speaker on Biblical topics having worked with thousands of individuals across the globe on topics including relationships, marriage and hearing God's voice. She is the host of "Conquering Our Unseen Enemies" Podcast and as a lifelong world traveler, she is the YouTube host of "Life Journey with Dawn Simmons." Over the course of her life, she has visited numerous archaeological and biblical sites which fueled her passion to help individuals understand biblical history and how it relates to our lives today. With education and research in both Business and History, including 20 years of mentoring and teaching, Dawn's coaching methodology helps people to better understand the Bible and develop their relationship with Jesus. Dawn is a mother of 4 and lives with her husband in Ventura County California.

Connect with us!

For more resources on how to develop your relationship with the Lord using the **SALO** method, join the SALO Circle membership community at our website:

www.lovingconversationssalo.com

Contact us at:
contact@lovingconversationssalo.com
Follow us on Instagram:
lovingconversationssalo

Related Titles:
Loving Conversations: How to Pray and Hear God's Voice
ISBN: 978-1-960775-05-4
Loving Conversations Study Guide and Journal: How to Pray and Hear God's Voice
ISBN: 978-1-960775-06-1
God's Promises SALO Devotional for Men
ISBN: 978-1-960